WORLDS APART

THEORY AND DECISION LIBRARY

General Editors: W. Leinfellner and G. Eberlein

Series A: Philosophy and Methodology of the Social Sciences
Editors: W. Leinfellner (Technical University of Vienna)
G. Eberlein (Technical University of Munich)

Series B: Mathematical and Statistical Methods
Editor: H. Skala (University of Paderborn)

Series C: Game Theory, Mathematical Programming and
Operations Research
Editor: S. H. Tijs (University of Nijmegen)

Series D: System Theory, Knowledge Engineering and Problem
Solving
Editor: W. Janko (University of Economics, Vienna)

SERIES A: PHILOSOPHY AND METHODOLOGY OF THE SOCIAL SCIENCES

Volume 14

Editors: W. Leinfellner (Technical University of Vienna)
G. Eberlein (Technical University of Munich)

Editorial Board

Scope

This series deals with the foundations, the general methodology and the criteria, goals and purpose of the social sciences. The emphasis in the new Series A will be on well-argued, thoroughly analytical rather than advanced mathematical treatments. In this context, particular attention will be paid to game and decision theory and general philosophical topics from mathematics, psychology and economics, such as game theory, voting and welfare theory, with applications to political science, sociology, law and ethics.

For a list of titles published in this series, see final page.

RICHARD L. DUKES

University of Colorado, Colorado Springs

WORLDS APART

*Collective Action in Simulated
Agrarian and Industrial Societies*

KLUWER ACADEMIC PUBLISHERS

DORDRECHT / BOSTON / LONDON

ISBN 0–7923–0620–1

Published by Kluwer Academic Publishers,
P.O. Box 17, 3300 AA Dordrecht, The Netherlands.

Kluwer Academic Publishers incorporates
the publishing programmes of
D. Reidel, Martinus Nijhoff, Dr W. Junk and MTP Press.

Sold and distributed in the U.S.A. and Canada
by Kluwer Academic Publishers,
101 Philip Drive, Norwell, MA 02061, U.S.A.

In all other countries, sold and distributed
by Kluwer Academic Publishers Group,
P.O. Box 322, 3300 AH Dordrecht, The Netherlands.

Printed on acid-free paper

To Cindy and the boys

who inspired me to get serious about play

HELPMATES

A large project like this one cannot be completed without the willing help of many people.

Sarane Spence Boocock taught me that learning could be fun. Sarane, Connie Seidner and Jeanne Curran taught me that being a student could be fun. They were the inspiration. Ed Ransford and Dan Glaser were instrumental in encouraging me to communicate to sociologists and other social scientists, not just to gamers. It is for them that the book is written.

The National Science Foundation provided funding for the gathering of the first part of the data set (GS34867), and the University of Colorado provided a summer fellowship at a critical juncture of the research. Dean James A. Null at the University of Colorado, Colorado Springs provided support at numerous times during the project. R. Garry Shirts, creator of the STARPOWER simulation, provided encouragement. It seemed that I was always telling him I'd be finished "next month."

Special thanks are due Cindy Dukes for help in innumerable areas of a study like this one in which thinking clearly is the prerequisite.

Nancy Ratledge helped prepare materials on the INTERNATIONAL SIMULATION. Sandra Matthews helped in many ways including organizing literature (with Robert Rossitto), coding, and data entry--all those tasks so necessary to a research that do not appear in the final write-up.

Chris Mattley's interest in STARPOWER for her master's thesis encouraged me to rededicate myself to the gathering of a data set that was large enough for the work I envisioned.

Assistance in the data gathering was provided by the following persons:

Cindy Dukes	Priscilla Nielsen
Sharon Littrell	Nancy Ratledge
Chris Mattley	Tom Segadey
Sandra Matthews	Pat Walker

This aspect of the project clearly is the one which was the most fun, but also it is one which often is overlooked by those who see only the final product.

Jay Coakley provided support and encouragement, and his students figured prominently in many of the games that are discussed herein.

Bob Hughes was always ready to discuss various aspects of the project, and he helped me more than he knows.

I would like to thank the following instructors for their help:

Jay Abarbanel	Barbara Mandell
Charles Bloch	Richard Mitchell
Jay Coakley	Mike Palmer
Jack Dyer	Jaime Raigoza
Joan Ginepra	Ed Ransford
Phil Gray	Harvey Rich
Al Himmelson	David Schneider
Chuck Hohm	Bernard Thorsell
Harvey Hyman	Mike Victor
Ken Johnson	Sylvia Weishaus
Sharon Littrell	Marcia Westkott
Scott Manard	Frances Yampolsky

Fred Goodman, Bill Gamson, Jon Turner and Mary Bredemeier provided direction and encouragement. Harry Bredemeier and Shirley Smoyak read earlier drafts of the manuscript. Lee Schantz read the final copy. Dora Donley, Penny Rinne, Lynn Scott, Pam Sherrow, and Peggy Reid typed earlier drafts of the manuscript. Joy Sanderson produced the printed figures. Special thanks are due Elaine Schantz for her excellent editorial assistance and for production of the final copy. She helped me to get it done!

Finally, I would like to thank the 1,200 students who participated in the games. Had the entire project been simulated, a more congenial and competent group of people could not have been created. It was fun!

Richard L. Dukes
Colorado Springs, Colorado

TABLE OF CONTENTS

LIST OF FIGURES

WORLDS APART

CHAPTER ONE

GAMED SIMULATIONS
FOR SOCIAL SCIENTISTS

On July 14, 1789, over 7000 Parisians took thousands of muskets from the Hôtel des Invalides and answered the call, "To the Bastille!" They were looking for powder which had been moved to the Bastille from a nearby armory, and the large guns mounted on the walls eighty feet above the ground were a threat to the densely populated tenements which surrounded the Bastille. Those guns were never fired, and assisted by Gardes Françaises and a few cannon, the Parisians stormed and took the Bastille. A decisive step had been taken in the French Revolution.

GAMING IN THE
COLLEGE CLASSROOM

Two hundred years after the French Revolution, a college student hurried from a history examination into her social science class. Unavoidably late, she arrived just in time to see half of the students jump up from their chairs in one part of the room to rush over and surround a tightly formed circle of seated classmates on the other side of the room. The standing students linked hands forming a human chain, completely encircling their surprised classmates. When the seated students tried to talk, those who were standing shouted them down and grabbed some white envelopes which they had been holding, spilling colored chips on the floor. The scene reminded the "late student" of the storming of the Bastille, but why were her normally tranquil classmates clashing like the eighteenth-century Parisians?

A few minutes later, she learned that the class had been playing STARPOWER, a game which creates conditions which are conducive to antagonistic encounters such as the storming of the Bastille, student protests in Berkeley or China, or revolution in Iran or the Philippines. Actually, the game is used to teach students about social class systems, but the systematic study of the game over many runs allows social scientists to gain a new perspective on these encounters that is unavailable through other methods.

1

SCIENTIFIC GAMING

This book explores scientific gaming, an interdisciplinary area of social science. No doubt most readers are familiar with parlor games such as MONOPOLY. Certainly, a fantasy game such as DUNGEONS AND DRAGONS is better known than is STARPOWER. Electronic games are played in virtually every urban area of the world. Who among these game players would recognize the names, SIMSOC (a gamed simulation about society), BAFA' BAFA' (a gamed simulation about intercultural contact), or GHETTO (a gamed simulation about the innercity)?

Despite the fact that the area of scientific gaming has a long history in academia and its own research journal, *Simulation and Games*, many readers still may be unfamiliar with it. They may be surprised to learn of the existence of over two-thousand academic games which have potential uses in scientific gaming (see Horn and Cleaves, 1980).

GAMED SIMULATION

This book is concerned with gamed simulations. They are games which have as their object the gaining of new insights into the selected aspects of the real social world which they mirror. These characteristics separate them from parlor games which do not make as determined an effort to represent reality. Gamed simulations do not require the extensive ability to make believe that is characteristic of fantasy games, but like fantasy games, most gamed simulations depend on an administrator who cooperates with players to make the game work. Gamed simulations differ from most electronic games in the area of social interaction. Players in gamed simulations provide the critical human features of the simulated environment that often are missing in the arcade. STARPOWER, the gamed simulation which this book is about, has not become a household word because, like most gamed simulations, it requires at least ten players and an administrator, so it has not been played widely outside of an educational context.

SOCIAL SCIENCE RESEARCH
WITH GAMED SIMULATIONS

The object of social science research with gamed simulations is the study of player behavior and the patterns of social organization which emerge within the simulated environments which gamed simulations create. Thus, gamed simulations provide contexts for testing theories about the real world. Among their many worthwhile qualities, foremost is their ability to abstract only the most important features of the phenomena which they model and to allow the replication of these features in a virtually unlimited number of runs. This feature will appeal to even the most hardnosed quantitative researcher. On the other hand, like their more popular relatives, gamed simulations first and foremost are fun, and this aspect makes research with them particularly appealing to qualitative researchers who emphasize human meaning and understanding. Gamed simulations stimulate a playful approach to inquiry which Phillips (1973) has argued, allow[s] us to confront our own experience, to pay attention to what we have seen, heard, felt and wondered about, and to what we already know. . . . Play may not only give reign to imagination, intuition, and creative urges, but may help us to see more clearly (Phillips, 1973: 162-165).

GAMES VERSUS REAL LIFE

The book is titled, *Worlds Apart* in order to emphasize the fact that the world of gamed simulation and the world of "real life" are not the same. On one hand, gamed simulations create social systems that are abstracted from the social world as a whole, and play within these systems, as Coleman (1968a) has said, is sort of a "time out" from the rest of social life. On the other hand as Wolf argues, games assert their own reality which is more important than real life. She says,

> Because of the immediacy of the situation, the game experience becomes larger than real life and occupies the whole field of societal perception (Wolf, 1972: 67).

This otherworldliness of gamed simulations is not a fault, because the gaming experience for players is real even though players are transported from a world with which they are familiar to one with which they are not.

THE INDUSTRIAL REVOLUTION

Europeans of the late eighteenth century saw the replacement of an order based on kinship and land by one based upon power and industry. Hobsbawm writes that the industrial revolution is,

> the greatest transformation in human history since the remote times when men invented agriculture and metallurgy, writing, the city and the state (Hobsbawm, 1962: 17).

These truly millennial changes have not been consolidated on a global level in the almost 250 years since the industrial revolution began. Both the magnitude and the pervasiveness of the industrial revolution have captured the attention of scholars in almost every discipline, and their writings are rich in imagery concerning the world before industrialization and the one which replaced it. This thought has yielded two almost polar opposite ideal types of societies, industrial and agrarian, which form the basis of research reported in this volume.

A second reason for calling this book *Worlds Apart* is to emphasize the tremendous differences between these two types of societies. The gamed simulation, STARPOWER, has been modified to create the social class systems of these two divergent worlds. Since no agrarian or industrial societies ever have existed in a pure form, simulation offers an opportunity to study them which is not possible using other methodologies.

STARPOWER

The gamed simulation, STARPOWER, models the stratification system of a society. The first play of the game produced a near riot, says R. Garry Shirts, its creator, and "the game has been going very well since then" (Coppard and Goodman, 1977: 306). His comments represent somewhat of an understatement, since STARPOWER probably is the all time most widely played gamed simulation.

The game models social processes that are of great interest to social scientists in the study of class systems and antagonistic encounters in both agrarian and industrial societies. STARPOWER creates a situation in which players strive to become (and to remain) members of the upper class. Mobility between classes takes place, and upper class members are given the complete authority to make the rules. Often this authority is used to repress the lower class. Repression may provide the impetus for it to organize and rebel against the rulemakers. In fact, it was this part of the game into which our "late student" walked at the beginning of the chapter.

RESEARCH DESIGN

Research with the game involves two versions of STARPOWER that are created by manipulation of the rules. One version represents an agrarian type of society that is characterized by ascribed status and low possibility of mobility. The other version of the game represents an industrial type of society which is characterized by achieved status and a higher possibility of mobility. The idea of a fixed volume of trade and wealth in the agrarian type is replaced by one of "unlimited progress in a free and expanding economy" which Ashton (1948: 22) cites as the central feature of the industrial type.

Findings reported in this volume are based upon sixty-four runs of STARPOWER. Thirty-two of the runs represented an agrarian type of society, and thirty-two runs represented an industrial type of society.

STRATIFICATION IN AGRARIAN AND
INDUSTRIAL SOCIETY CONTRASTED

France of the late eighteenth century still was an agrarian society, and one of the important factors in the revolution was a peasant demand for land, a fixed asset controlled by the gentry. Compare these fixed assets to variable ones which are generated in the market for new products in modern nations. In the late nineteen-seventies, Steve Jobs, the son of a machinist, sold his Volkswagen bus, so he and a friend could start Apple Computers. He was the largest stockholder in the corporation, and his success was mercurial.

When asked about it, Steve said,

> I was worth a million dollars on paper when I was twenty-three, ten million when I was twenty-four, and a hundred million when I was twenty-five. I had several years to figure out what I thought about all this stuff before it got to epidemic proportions (Gardner, 1984: 21-22).

An open opportunity structure in the society plus plenty of talent and hard work allowed Jobs to succeed, but what about those who do not? In *Hidden Injuries of Class*, Sennett and Cobb (1972) found that those who do not succeed blame themselves more than they blame the system of stratification. Individuals who compete successfully are apt to keep on competing, and the "injured" are unlikely to engage in antagonistic encounters with them.

Had our "late student" walked into the classroom at the same point in the industrial version of STARPOWER, she might have seen players trading furiously with whoever was nearest to them in order to earn as many points as possible. She even might have seen a Steve Jobs.

By the late nineteen-eighties Steve had been removed from his position at Apple, and he was in the process of launching another company. This removal was similar to a process in STARPOWER whereby a player can be expelled from a group by a majority vote of the players in it. Expulsion can happen in either the agrarian or the industrial version of the game, but the consequences are dire in the agrarian version because of the closed nature of the opportunity structure. Once someone loses a position in the upper class, recovery is almost impossible because additional points are so difficult to earn. In the industrial version of STARPOWER, an expelled player may just "start another company."

The emphasis on individuals of this discussion may have obscured the richness of their collective interactions in the antagonistic encounters that are generated in STARPOWER. The examination of collective action is the focus of the entire project, and the patterns of conflict and change which took place in the simulated societies are quite interesting.

FINDINGS ABOUT CONFLICT AND CHANGE

Eleven of the sixty-four simulated societies underwent drastic change. In four of the eleven societies, the upper class members completely repressed the lower class by ending the game. In three of the eleven societies the upper class group collapsed. In four of the eleven societies, the lower class members rebelled by erasing the blackboard, taking chips of the upper class members, or by preventing them from trading through physical restraint. Of the eleven societies which underwent drastic change, nine were of the agrarian type and two were of the industrial type.

The type of society is the framework within which all other activity takes place. Like the storming of the Bastille, real stories are contained in the events which led up to the collective encounters and in the ones which followed them. For instance, three weeks before the storming of the Bastille, the Estates General declared resolutions of the widely popular National Assembly to be null and void. The feudal system was to remain intact. Rioting broke out all over the city. Then three days before Bastille, the head of the National Assembly was sent into exile, and a full scale insurrection lasting several days featured the search for arms. It set the stage for the famous encounter of July 14.

Had our "late student" entered the classroom five minutes earlier, she might have heard members of the lower class asking the upper class rulemakers to increase the value of the lowest chips. She would have seen them write the new rule that forbade lower class members to trade with each other. She would have understood more fully the context in which the lower class students organized themselves and surrounded their classmates. And she would have been struck by the similarity between what was happening in her social science course and events in the world outside the classroom, because like the French Revolution, after the collective action the society was changed fundamentally, and the social classes never again returned to patterns that were established in earlier times.

WHAT IS A GAMED SIMULATION?

A gamed simulation is a unique combination of a game and a simulation that profits from its hybrid nature. Games may be thought of as activities in which interactions by players are given meaning. Suits (1967) has identified the process by which meaning is created. He concludes that to play a game is,

> to engage in activity directed toward bringing about a specific state of affairs, using only means permitted by specific rules, where the means permitted by the rules are more limited in scope than they would be in the absence of the rules, and where the sole reason for accepting such limitations is to make possible such activity (Suits, 1967: 156).

Competition is not a necessary condition for a game, but usually goal attainment is structured by the rules so that competition (and perhaps also cooperation) becomes a vehicle for it. Games, then, are activities which have goals and rules. As such, they are not easily distinguishable from many other facets of social life.

Games as Analogies
To Real Life

Huizinga (1955) characterizes humans as players and culture as the arena. Long (1958) has described the human community as an ecology of games. McCain and Segal (1969) have depicted science as a game, and Berne (1964) portrays the game qualities of social interaction. In identifying a game as a "caricature of social life," Coleman ably describes these links.

> . . . a game is a . . . play upon life in general, it induces, in a restricted and well-defined context, the same kinds of motivations and behaviors that occur in the broader contexts of life where we play for keeps (Coleman, 1968b: 29).

Variables and Constants

The link between games and the real world is conceptualized more adequately as a constant than as a variable for a particular socio-cultural context. Social reality in some cultures is more gamelike than it is in others. By operating the game within a single cultural context, the effect is held constant. In the simulation part of gamed simulations the relation of the gamed simulation to its referent system becomes a variable. It is in this area that the validity of a simulation takes on its proper meaning.

Nominal and Real Definitions

Another way to present the distinction between game and simulation is to adopt Bierstedt's solution to the nominalist/realist debate.

> A nominal definition (sometimes called a verbal definition) "is a declaration of intention to use a certain word of phrase as a substitute for another word or phrase" (Bierstedt, 1959: 131 quoting Easton, 1933: 295).

The game aspect of gamed simulation may be likened to a nominal definition. The measure of a game is its utility, its ability to generate a more or less closed system of meaning for players. The game itself makes no truth claims. It does not assert anything about some referent system. The fact that games in general have meaning within a social system is important, but it is not the crucial issue.

On the other hand, real definitions make truth claims. They assert something about the referent. They are a product of research. In a real definition,

> we no longer want to know what the word stands for in terms of other symbols, but what the referent of the concept is, in terms of other symbols, and what its properties are--especially those properties that enable us to use *this* word, with its own independent meaning, as a terminological and logical equivalent (Bierstedt, 1959: 131; italics appear in the original text).

The simulation aspect of a gamed simulation is closer to the notion of real definitions than is the game aspect. These distinctions are outlined in Figure 1-1.

Autotelic Behavior: Game

The analytical distinction between games and play often is made as a way in which to simplify the definition of play. Inbar (1970) felt that the "play aspect" of gamed simulations must be made clear, or the whole definition of games breaks down. He proposed the concept of autotelic behavior as a way of dealing with this problem. Autotelic behavior is "engaged in for its own sake." As such, "it constitutes an end in itself" (Inbar, 1970: 1; this discussion also may be found in Inbar and Stoll, 1970). The concept of autotelic behavior is approached on three levels: formal characteristics of games (which were discussed above), psychological definitions of games, and social definitions of games.

8

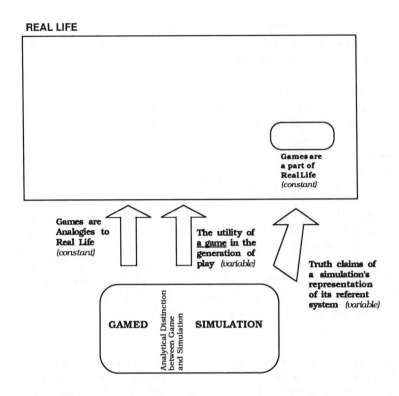

REAL LIFE

Games are
a part of
Real Life
(constant)

Games are
Analogies to
Real Life
(constant)

The utility of
a game in the
generation of
play *(variable)*

Truth claims of
a simulation's
representation
of its referent
system *(variable)*

GAMED   Analytical Distinction between Game and Simulation   SIMULATION

Figure 1-1: Distinctions Between Real Life and Gamed Simulations

Autotelic Behavior: Game Situation

When a player has accepted a game psychologically,

> only by respecting the rules is there meaning in the activity. Hence, the psychological
> disposition elicited is to accept as binding whatever rules define the game. This is
> the essence of the "play spirit" . . . the goal has acquired an intrinsic value
> independent of the constraints (Inbar, 1970: 6).

The social definition of a game involves separating game events from the business
of life. Figure 1-2 illustrates Inbar's point of view. The concept of autotelic
behavior explains similarities between games and many other social situations
(even wars, for instance) which have similar formal characteristics. It explains how
some games can lose the play spirit and become deadly serious when valuable
payoffs are a result of winning, i.e., the social definition of the game becomes
similar to other activities in life. It also explains how games spring up in many
"serious" social situations when participants adopt a play spirit which overcomes
the prevailing social definitions of seriousness.

GAME (The objective observer's perspective)		GAME SITUATION (Subjective perspective of players)
FORMAL CHARACTERISTICS Set of Rules which: 1. Define the Goal 2. Set up constraints in goal attainment process.	SOCIAL DEFINITION Society: 1. Defines goal as inconsequential to the serious business of life. 2. Defines activities of game as inconsequential to the serious business of life.	PSYCHOLOGICAL CHARACTERISTICS Players: 1. View goal as unrelated to serious aspects of "real world" 2. Accept constraints as binding on one's activities within the game (play spirit) Result: goal has acquired an intrinsic value independent of constraints (expectation of fun or interest)

Figure 1-2: **Characteristics of Autotelic Behavior (Inbar, 1970; Inbar and Stoll, 1970)**

SIMULATION

Raser (1969) has made the connection between the term "simulation" and other, more traditional scientific activities. He says that "Simulation is, in essence, the process of analogizing. So is all science" (Raser, 1969: XI). The analogy is necessarily limited, since the entire system is not represented in a simulation. Some aspects are simplified, and others are left out.

> [T]he model does not have to *look like* the referent system, but should *behave* like it (Greenblat, 1988: 52; italics appear in the original).

As implied in the above quote, unlike verbal theories, simulations are models which operate.

> A model is a specific form of theory, so a simulation is a specific variety of model, distinguished by the fact that a simulation is a dynamic or operating model (Crow, as quoted in Raser, 1969: 9).

Scientific Paradigms:
Clarity and Consensus

Fred Goodman (personal communication) has proposed continuua of clarity and consensus, that are used to limit the scope of simulation. For the phenomena being modeled, the clarity continuum runs from general modes of action (low clarity) to formal codes of action (high clarity). The consensus continuum runs from an individual idiosyncratic view of principles thought to govern a phenomenon (low consensus) to a widespread acceptance of a particular set of principles in governing a phenomenon (high consensus). These continuua are cross classified to form a 2 x 2 table (see Figure 1-3). When clarity is high, a simplified working model may not be needed for understanding and control of a phenomenon. When consensus is high, principles are generally agreed upon, so simulation is not necessary to uncover them. When both clarity and consensus are high, the term "non-simulation" best describes the logically closed, highly accepted situation that is similar to the rules of mathematics.

CLARITY

	Low	High
High	Conventional Wisdom (eg. phenomonology)	Non-Simulation (eg. rules of Math, law of gravity)
Low	SIMULATION	Controversial Theory (eg. evolution)

CONSENUS

Figure 1-3   Goodman's Clarification of the Term, "Simulation."

Simulation is the preferred method of study when our understanding lacks both clarity and consensus. Goodman's use of "clarity and consensus" is similar to Thomas Kuhn's (1970) concept of "scientific paradigm," which is based on,

> achievements that some particular scientific community acknowledged for a time [consensus] as supplying the foundation for its further practice [clarity] (Kuhn, 1970: 10; material in square brackets added for emphasis).

Social science is an ideal arena on the practice of simulation, since it is characterized by low clarity and low consensus.

GAMED SIMULATIONS

In gamed simulations, the autotelic behavior that is characteristic of games is used to operate the simulation model. As Seidner (1978) says,

> . . . the parameters of the referent system are embedded in a set of specifications, or rules, that define the roles and resources of participants. These specifications are devised to reflect the restraints inherent in the referent system so that simulation

participants will experience some of the same kinds of pressures and influences that would occur in a real-life setting (Seidner, 1978: 16).

Lauffer (1973) captures the essence of the gamed simulation in a different way. He says that gamed simulations are abstractions.

Players act within a social environment . . . representing people, groups, organizations, social and economic forces . . . governed by certain rules that permit its responses to be contingent on the actions of individuals. . . . Participants play, but they make believe for real (Lauffer, 1973: 21).

In the vignette at the beginning of the chapter it was this unique combination of play and abstraction that brought the reality of the French Revolution to the college classroom.

CHAPTER TWO

HISTORY OF GAMED SIMULATION
IN SOCIAL SCIENCE RESEARCH

Gamed simulations have been used by social scientists in two major ways. First, they have been used to investigate the operation of social systems through the study of the behavior of players within them, and second, they have been used to teach students about the characteristics of the social systems that are modeled by the games.

The use of gamed simulations to study social systems was begun by the Internation Simulation (INS) Project at Northwestern University in the 1960's. Under the leadership of Harold Guetzkow, the goal of the INS Project was to investigate issues of war and peace such as the impact on the international system of the spread of nuclear weapons to countries which previously had only non-nuclear capability. Using students as subjects, the INS researchers systematically varied the proliferation of nuclear weapons, and then they observed the frequency and severity of international conflict. The research represented an extension of the laboratory experiment from social psychology. It was performed outside of the college classroom, and no attempt was made to link the curriculum to the research effort. The technique was successful in testing social science theories of international conflict, as testified by findings that are reviewed below.

The second major use of gamed simulation was exemplified by the Academic Games Project at Johns Hopkins University in the late 1960's and early 1970's. Under the leadership of James Coleman, the Hopkins Group investigated the effects of playing a game upon cognitive and affective outcomes among student players. Typically, the research setting was the classroom, and the investigators extended the curriculum to include games. Conclusions from over 150 studies conducted by the Hopkins Group were that gamed simulations as teaching devices could be at least as effective as more traditional methods (see Livingston, Fennessey, Coleman, Edwards and Kidder, 1973).

Figure 2-1 summarizes the ways in which gamed simulations have been used in research. The figure shows both Hopkins-type research and Northwestern-type research. The primary difference between them is the dependent variable. In Hopkins-type research the dependent variable is personal change in players that persists after the exercise is over. Typically, this variable is motivation, cognitive or affective learning, creativity, or competence. The work has been reviewed effectively by Bredemeier and Greenblat (1981) and by Seidner (1978).

14

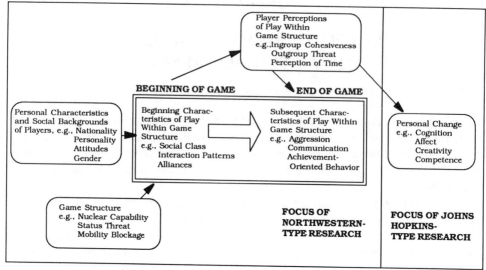

Figure 2-1: General Model for Research with Gamed Simulations

Northwestern-type research involves the use of a dependent variable that is focused on the game itself, such as the behavior of players or at least their perceptions of play. The type of research with which this book will be concerned is a combination of both the Northwestern and Hopkins types. Its aims are the same as those of the Northwestern type, but it makes use of the classroom as a setting for the simulation. As such, it combines both the research and teaching emphases, but student learning is not evaluated. Since research in this book is concerned with collective action, research from studies of the Northwestern type will be reviewed.

Technically, all of the studies that are presented in the chapter are validity studies whether or not they were thought of as such by their authors. Perhaps the most powerful form of validity is theoretical validity in which the criterion against which a game is judged is social science theory. If a game is valid, behavior within it should be similar to that which is predicted from the theory. Can research both test a theory and establish the validity of the method to make the test? There is no reason why it can't, and the case for doing so is strengthened by the fact that collective action theory is tested in other contexts such as laboratory experiments, surveys and case studies.

INTER-NATION SIMULATION (INS)

Clearly, the most well developed program of research using a single gamed simulation was completed by Guetzkow and his colleagues at Northwestern University. For almost a decade, the INTER-NATION SIMULATION was the setting for studies on international conflict by this group. A complete summary of over twenty years of research appears in Guetzkow and Valdez (1981).

Inter-Nation Simulation (INS) (Guetzkow, Alger, Brody, Noel and Synder, 1963) consists of seven nations and the relations among them. The nations of INS do not correspond to particular real world nations *per se* (e.g., France), but the seven nations do share common features with each other that are similar to actual nations in terms of relative wealth and power. Nations are divided into internal and external sectors. Two or more decision makers within each nation allocate resources into these sectors in order to achieve national goals (e.g., growth, security, etc.).

The roles within each nation consist of (1) a "central decision-maker," the chief-of-state, who performs the executive function of government, (2) one or two "external decision-makers" who represent the foreign relations structure of the nation and who perform this function, and (3) one or more "aspiring decision-makers" who represent leaders of competing elites in the nation who seek to gain office.

In addition to its decision-makers, each nation has a set of validators, i.e., individuals or power groups within a nation to whom the decision-makers are responsible. If validators are satisfied, they will support the central decision-maker in office. Dissatisfaction leads to their support of one of the aspiring decision-makers. These validators are not actual players. They exist only on the conceptual level. Validator satisfaction is derived from indicators of standard of living and national security (see Sullivan and Noel, 1972, for a complete review of the characteristics of INS). The most important feature of the exercise is that conventional or nuclear war can break out among the simulated nations. This aspect of INS has led to eight major studies.

Brody (1963)

In this research, Brody created two hierarchically organized bloc alliances. The commanding nations in each bloc possessed nuclear strike and counter-strike capabilities. As other nations within the blocs obtained nuclear arms, Brody hypothesized that fragmentation within blocs would result. This fragmentation would be the result of an increased sense of independence and a lowering of the perceived threat from the opposing bloc by previously non-nuclear nations.

To test his fragmentation hypothesis, the INS model was restructured in the following manner: (1) Two new nations were added to increase the possible number of dyads. (2) Force capabilities were differentiated into nuclear and conventional. Nuclear weapons were considered to be more effective against certain targets, but they were more expensive to produce. (3) The concept of research and development was introduced into INS in order to add a plausible cover for the experimental intervention, the introduction of nuclear force capabilities (Brody, 1963).

The participants were high school students from North Shore and North Chicago high schools. Equal numbers of males and females were selected for the study. Students also were selected on a concrete-abstract personality dimension. Nations were made up of similar personality types, and nation-personality type combinations were randomized across runs. A total of 357 students participated in the runs. Analysis of data that were generated by these INS runs revealed that four key changes resulted from the spread of nuclear capability: (1) threat external to the bloc of nations was reduced, (2) threat internal to the bloc was increased, (3) cohesiveness of the blocs was reduced, and (4) bipolarity between the blocks was lessened. In general, the alliances between individual nations which formed the international blocs were weakened, and the blocs themselves seemed less likely to engage in conflict with each other.

Crow and Raser (1964)

These two investigators studied the effects of the ability of a nation to delay a nuclear response on perceived strength, the outbreak of war, and arms control. The research involved a cross-cultural setting. Eleven runs of the simulation were conducted with U.S. Naval recruits who recently had completed basic training in the top twenty-five percent of their class. Two runs of the simulation were conducted with second year college students in Mexico.

Nations which could delay their responses were seen as stronger and more threatening than those which could not do so. In the U.S. data the chances of accidental war were seen as less likely if a nation could delay its response. Capacity for a delayed response did not affect the desire of a nation to reach an arms control agreement, the ability of a nation to negotiate more adequately, deterrence, alliance cohesion, magnitude of war, or the probability of war. In short, delayed response was shown to be a worthwhile capability of a nation.

When U.S. players and Mexican players were compared, the latter communicated more often and more formally (e.g., emphasis on grammar), emphasized international issues, de-emphasized internal growth, shared power more readily with other countries, and reacted more passively to stress and frustration.

This rather limited cross-cultural investigation suggests that the cultural background of participants is an important variable in gamed simulation as well as in the real world. It deserves much more attention than it has received in research with gamed simulations.

Driver (1965)

This study investigated the effects of stress and personality structure on perceptions and aggression. The same sixteen runs of the simulation used by Brody (1963) provided the data that were used in Driver's research.

The purpose of the study was to interpret the relationship between stress (the spread of nuclear arms) and aggression (war in INS). Driver found that the less complicated were the cognitive structures of decision makers (either due to personality or to stress factors) the more likely was aggression. The simplification of a decision maker's thinking involved: "(1) loss of nonaggressive alternatives to war, (2) simplification of perception in which deterrence awareness [was] increasingly blurred (Driver, 1965: 13)."

The simulation runs contained some nations of decision-makers who systematically differed in personality along the abstract-concrete dimension. Driver found that,

> Abstract level groups . . . avoid serious aggression, particularly war. . . . The picture for concrete groups is nearly reversed. Concreteness in personality organization implies the occurrence of some kind of aggression (Driver, 1965: 40-41).

Driver developed the analysis by including measurements of distrust as measured by the California F-scale and by theorizing extensively upon the operation of various intervening variables which interpreted the relationships between independent and dependent variables. Driver summarized his findings by stating that,

> War requires a stress of arms increase which so concretizes cognitive structure that serious aggression is a probable response. . . . [S]erious aggression is frequent among concrete groups and is almost always found in concrete groups with high distrust (Driver, 1965: 43).

Brody, Benham and Milstein (1966)

This team used data from the INS runs in order to investigate the process of an arms race. Specifically, they investigated the intervening mechanism by which expressed hostility and military buildup on the part of one nation produced the observed reciprocal behavior on the part of an adversary. Brody *et al.* summarized their findings by stating that,

> We have found that hostile behavior is in general a product both of hostile behavior and of perceptions of that behavior, and that a variety of elements such as salience, capability, threat, and perceived qualities of the external nation are involved in accounting for hostile action (Brody, *et al.*, 1966: 79).

Zinnes (1966)

Four key questions prompted the investigation by Zinnes of hostile behavior of decision-makers in simulate and historical data. The questions were: What factors affect a decision-maker's perception of his environment? What are some of the consequences of these perceptions of hostility? Are there differences in perception and overt behavior between high school decision-makers and national decision-makers? What does a comparison of historical and simulate data suggest about the prospects for the further simulation of international behavior in the laboratory?

Thirteen hypotheses were tested in order to answer these broad questions. Data were provided by two sources: INS runs and documents and communications among six major state participants in the six-week crises in Europe prior to the outbreak of World War I. Her four principal variables were:

18

perception of threat, perception of unfriendliness, expression of hostility, and frequency of interaction. Figure 2-2 presents the interrelationships among the various parts of the model. The relationships among the parts of the model generally were supported by both sets of data.

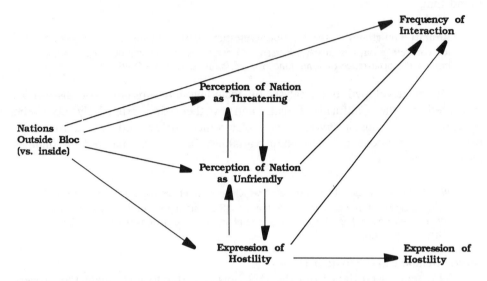

Figure 2-2: Relationships That Were Tested by Zinnes (1966) Using Both Historical
and Simulate Data

Hermann and Hermann (1967)

This pair of investigators also used INS to simulate the international political situation prior to the First World War. Five nations were simulated: Austria-Hungary, England, France, Germany, and Russia. Five major modifications were made to the INS model. They included: 1) establishing the initial conditions which characterized the international situation in the summer of 1914 by way of a brief history presented prior to play, 2) a statement of current domestic and foreign policies of each nation, 3) an attempt to match personality traits of the players to the historical policy maker role which was assumed by each participant, and 4) a set of relevant messages, conversations and newspapers from the preceding weeks. In addition to these changes, parameters of INS such as basic and force capabilities, validator satisfaction and decision latitude were changed in the simulation to match those of the countries involved. Events reported in historical accounts and general hypotheses about political events were compared to play.

The final day in the simulation represented the day in history when Austria-Hungary declared war on Serbia. That point was not reached when the simulation was terminated, but hostility was present, and in the debriefing sessions, participants felt that war would have occurred during the next day or two of simulated time. In a second run, several major divergences from the outbreak of war developed. England took a stronger position earlier in the game, and the course of actual events was not followed. In the first run, all eighteen events reported in the historical data were matched to actions in the simulation, and they were found to be similar in intent. Nine events were judged equivalent in physical format, and four events took place at approximately the same point in the game as they did in the real world. One explanation that was offered by the Hermanns for the discrepancies between the timing of some events in the simulation and those which actually took place prior to World War I was the difficulty in simulating real time accurately.

Two hypotheses of a more traditional type were tested with the simulation data. First, if a state's perception of injury to itself is sufficiently great, this perception would offset perceptions of insufficient capability. The decision to go to war would be made independently of the ability to wage war. This hypothesis was supported by the data. In the simulation, the perceptions of hostility were significantly greater than those of capability in both runs. Second, when opposing alliances or blocs emerge in the international politics of INS, the communication between blocs would be worded much weaker than that among alliance partners. Data from both runs supported this hypothesis, but the data from Run 2 were not statistically significant.

Druckman (1968)

Another example of research using the INS model for testing social theory can be seen in Druckman's study. At the end of each of eleven INS runs, participants were asked to rate all other participants *as persons* on several personality traits. He found strong support for the hypothesis that judgements will be more favorable to members of one's own nation than to outgroup members, allies, or enemies. Data also supported the hypothesis that judgements will be more favorable to members of allied nations than to members of enemy nations. Thus, ethnocentrism in the simulation was found to be a universal bias in favor of the members of one's own group.

Hermann (1972)

Hermann used INS to focus upon international crises. Ten separate runs of thirty players each were used to generate the data on the simulated crises. The players were Petty Officers in the United States Navy. Hermann defined a crisis in the following way.

> A situation [that] threatens one or more important goals of a state, . . . (2) allows only a short time for decision before the situation is significantly transformed, and (3) occurs as a surprise to the policy makers (Herman, 1972: 182).

The study incorporated three major crisis variables: threat, decision time, and surprise. Each of these variables was manipulated experimentally, and five types of perceptions of players were measured via responses to questionnaire items that were completed immediately after a crisis. Five dependent variables were measured in order to investigate the effects of crises on decision processes. They are presented in Figure 2-3. An additional variable of Nation was used in order to investigate whether certain combinations of resources, alliance membership, national goals, or status in the international system affected crisis behavior of the nation.

Dependent Variable	Operational Definition and Prediction
Contraction of Authority	Reduction in the number of decision makers who asume a major role in decision making
Number of Alternatives	The number of alternative solutions to the crisis will be reduced
Internal Communciation	The rate of communication by foreign policy agencies within a nation will increase
External Communication	The rate of communication by decision makers to international actors will increase
Frequency of Action	Frequency of action in response to crisis will increase

Figure 2-3: Dependent Variables for the Study by Hermann (1972)

None of the crisis variables produced consistent differences in dependent variables. Hermann speculated that the experimental differences were not great enough to create similar perceptions among players in similar treatment conditions, but player perceptions were predictive of decision making behavior despite the fact that these perceptions were produced by various types of crisis situations. The variable of *nation* appeared to interact with crisis variables in determining decision making processes.

SIMSOC (SIMULATED SOCIETY)

This gamed simulation has been played by more individuals and groups than any simulation except STARPOWER. Gamson has continued to improve the game since its development in the mid-sixties. He estimates that as of 1977 the game had been played by 5000 groups which included approximately 200,000 individuals (1978: Front matter).

SIMSOC models four geographical regions, seven basic groups, four national indicators, subsistence and travel agencies, and a bank. Many activities are available to players in SIMSOC. They can do things such as, solve problems, work and be unemployed, invest money, consume, join organizations, take political action, riot, go to jail, and die.

Research with SIMSOC

This exercise holds much promise for future research, since it mirrors a great number of macro-level processes. As with many of the gamed simulations to be discussed below, its research potential remains largely untapped. Studies by Silver (1973, 1974) represent first attempts to fulfill its promise.

Silver (1973)

Drawing heavily on Dahrendorf (1959), Silver tested a theoretical model that presented intergroup antagonism as a result of status threat and mobility blockage. Data were gathered from 140 student players of SIMSOC who were randomly assigned to one of the regions. Silver's analysis was based upon seventy-two players for whom complete data were available.

The independent variable of status threat was manipulated by telling members of Green region that they had the largest number of group heads (an advantage), but since they had not performed better in the game than the other groups, they would receive a lower grade for the exercise than would the others.

A second independent variable, mobility blockage, was manipulated by providing players in some regions with fewer subsistence and travel tickets than players in other regions received (a disadvantage). The dependent variable of intergroup antagonism was measured by the ratio of the number of arrests to the number of police forces initiated by each region, and by the number of arrests. SIMSOC data provided some support for the theoretical model.

Silver (1974)

In his second study with SIMSOC, Silver used the same data set, but the study was oriented differently. The dependent variable of the second study was the degree of commitment to the group to which a player had been assigned at the beginning of the game. Commitment was measured after the game by asking players which group they would have preferred to be in if they had been given a choice. The success of one's group in the maintenance of a productive society predicted one's commitment to the game group, but the degree of individual goal attainment that was defined by each player at the beginning of the game (e.g., to be wealthy, powerful, etc.) did not predict one's commitment to the group.

STARPOWER

Chapter Four is devoted to the discussion of STARPOWER. For now let it suffice to say that STARPOWER creates a system of stratification. Players within each class of the system have similar resources in the form of colored playing chips. Players in higher classes generally have more valuable chips. High scoring players can experience upward mobility. After several rounds, upper class players are given complete authority to make rules for subsequent rounds of the game. Sometimes lower class members refuse to obey the rules, and they engage in collective action that is similar to boycotts, general strikes, or rebellion.

Research with STARPOWER

STARPOWER lends itself to research in stratification, political decision making, and collective action. Research by Dukes (1974) and Dukes and Mattley (1986) are examples of the usage of the game in these areas. In a novel approach, Plummer (1976) used the game to create Future Shock (Toffler, 1970).

Dukes (1974)

This research used data from twenty-four runs of STARPOWER in order to test a theoretical model derived from Dahrendorf (see Figure 2-4).

Two different versions of the game were used in an experimental design. One version represented an open mobility system (Industrial type), and the other version represented a closed mobility system (Capitalistic type). The model involved the regulation of conflict in industrial societies. To the extent that classes were perceived by players as organized, individuals were perceived to be more involved in the game. Organization of the classes also led to the perception that

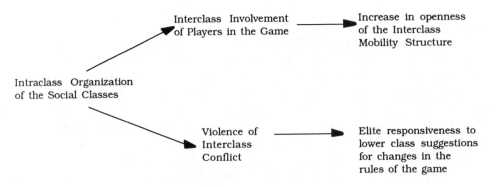

Figure 2-4: Theoretical Model tested by Dukes (1974)

23

conflict was less "violent." Perceived involvement of players tended to create pressure toward increased openness of the mobility structure, and non-violent conflict tended to create pressure within institutionalized channels resulting in elite responsiveness. The study predicted correctly that the Dahrendorf model would be supported by the data for the Industrial type societies, and the data would not support the model for the Capitalistic type societies, since in this latter type of society conflict tends to be expressed outside of institutional channels.

Dukes and Mattley (1986)

This research used an expanded data set that included the one used by Dukes (1974). It contained forty-eight plays of STARPOWER. The data were used to test a theoretical model of achievement oriented behavior (see Figure 2-5). Data from these plays supported the theoretical model. Open class systems were correctly perceived by players (especially by those who actually experienced mobility in the game). Perceptions of openness in the mobility structure produced achievement oriented behavior (trading) by players.

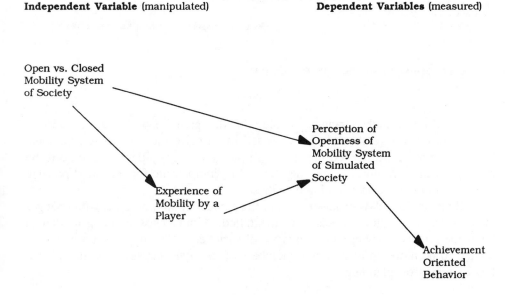

Independent Variable (manipulated)   **Dependent Variables** (measured)

Figure 2-5: Theoretical Model Tested by Dukes and Mattley (1986)

24

Plummer (1976)

This unique research used data from eight runs of STARPOWER in order to test a theoretical model based on Toffler's Future Shock, (1970) (see Figure 2-6). Two different versions of STARPOWER were used in the research. In one version, a rule was changed every thirty seconds in order to simulate a more rapidly changing society. In the other version, a rule was changed only every three minutes in order to simulate a less rapidly changing society.

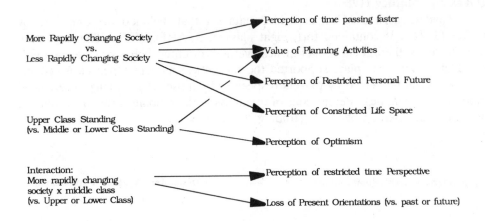

Figure 2-6 Theoretical Model Tested By Plummer (1976)

Players in the rapidly changing version of the game experienced a type of game-induced "future shock." They tended to perceive more restricted personal futures and more constricted life spaces in the game. They perceived time to be passing much more quickly, and they tended to compensate for the rapid passage of time by emphasizing planning activities.

Being middle class or lower class in the game tended to interact with changes in the rules; thus, these effects were magnified. Upper class standing tended to blunt the effects of change in both types of societies. Also, upper class members tended to be more optimistic than members of the other classes, and they placed less emphasis on planning.

HIGH SCHOOL

This game by Coleman and Seidner (1972) simulates the value climate in the school setting that was found by Coleman (1961) to be an important influence on student achievement. In the game, players are assigned to one of the six student profiles which vary in ability level for each of three common activities in a high school setting: Academics, Athletics, and Social Activities. Players invest their time in these activities in order to win achievement points. The amount of achievement that is won in an activity by a student is a function of both the student's ability and the amount of time that is invested in that activity. Achievement points bring players social and self esteem. Parents and friends are simulated reference groups in the game. The number of esteem points derived through them varies with the values that players place on achievement in an activity. The game presents three ideal-type school value climates by varying the weightings of parent and peer value systems. For instance, the value climate in the Green Junction school generally favors athletics. The one in Mid-City favors academics, and the value climate in Executive Heights favors social activities. The object of the game is to win as many esteem points as possible. The game contains a system of exchange which enables players to bargain for friendship and "help" in the acquisition of additional achievement from the other players during the game.

Russell (1972)

Russell varied the value climates of HIGH SCHOOL in order to simulate an academically oriented peer culture and a nonacademically oriented peer culture. The peer value climates were similar to Mid-City and Green Junction respectively. Parental value climates were held constant. Data were generated from twenty runs of the simulation. Findings from the simulation supported and extended Coleman's findings in the Adolescent Society.

The manipulated independent variable of peer value climate had a strong effect on academic achievement, as did the ability level of the student profile. Furthermore, the data exhibited an interaction effect between value climate and ability level upon academic achievement (see Figure 2-7). Russell summarized the study as follows:

> These findings suggest a relationship which can only be inferred from Coleman's data, that the correlation between effort (or time) expended in pursuing an activity and one's ability in that activity is highest for those activities that are most highly rewarded by the peer group (Russell, 1972: 174).

This interaction also affected a player's self-esteem. In both Coleman's and Russell's findings, "students whose personal attributes were not consonant with peer culture values tended to have lower self-evaluations than students whose attributes were highly valued by their peers (Russell, 1972: 175).

Dukes and Seidner (1973)

This research used data from nine runs of HIGH SCHOOL to investigate the interaction effects of personal characteristics and characteristics of the randomly assigned role in the game upon the degree of effectiveness of role enactment by the player.

Self-role incongruence resulted from differences between characteristics of a player and the characteristics of the role to which the player was assigned in the game. Two types of incongruence were created by the random assignment of

26

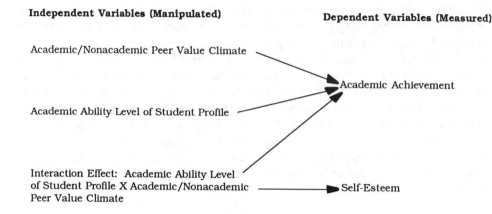

Independent Variables (Manipulated)

Dependent Variables (Measured)

Academic/Nonacademic Peer Value Climate

Academic Achievement

Academic Ability Level of Student Profile

Interaction Effect: Academic Ability Level
of Student Profile X Academic/Nonacademic — Self-Esteem
Peer Value Climate

Figure 2-7: Theoretical Model Tested By Russell (1972)

players to roles in the nine runs of HIGH SCHOOL. Sex incongruence occurred when a player was assigned a student profile of the opposite sex (e.g., John Doe is assigned to the role of Linda). Ability incongruence occurred when the abilities of the assigned student profile differed from a player's estimates of his own academic, athletic, and social abilities.

Effectiveness of role enactment was operationalized as game score, i.e., social and self esteem. Dissonance reduction was measured by categorizing players' post-game written suggestions on redesign of the game. The authors inferred that players reduced dissonance by redesigning the game in ways which eliminated the differences between self characteristics and the attributes of the roles to which they were assigned.

Results of the study indicated that self-role ability incongruence tended to decrease effective role enactment, while self-role sex incongruence had no strong main effect. The data indicated that sex incongruence may have interacted statistically with ability incongruence in its influence on effective role enactment. Ability incongruence also had a stronger effect on redesign categories than did sex incongruence.

Seidner and Dukes (1976)

This research used data from sixteen runs of HIGH SCHOOL to investigate the interactive effects of self values and those of reference groups upon achievement oriented behavior in the game. The theoretical model used in this research was developed within the more traditional research setting of the experimental laboratory (see Acock and DeFleur, 1972). Seidner and Dukes examined the predictive ability of the model within the context of a game simulation.

Results of the study supported the theoretical model. The interactive model predicted achievement-oriented behavior in the game better than did individual attitudes or an additive model of attitudes and reference group values.

GENERATION GAP

This two-person gamed simulation was developed by Boocock and Schild (1969). In the game players take on the role of either an adolescent or the teen's parent. Play focuses upon issues concerning the behavior of the adolescent, such as dating, helping around the house, personal appearance, school homework, and staying out late at night. Each issue is stated in two contradictory ways, for example:

(1) teen's favor: Teen will stay out late.
(2) parent's favor: Teen will be home by 10 o'clock.

Each player secretly weights each issue according to his values as 10, 8, 6, 4, or 2 points. Then the parent and the adolescent discuss which one of the two alternatives the adolescent will choose. If they cannot come to an agreement, the parent may "order" the adolescent to behave in a certain way. Next, the adolescent secretly "obeys or disobeys" on each issue. The teen wins his own value weightings for all those issues in which the behavior is in the teen's favor. The parent wins her own value weightings for all those issues in which the teen's behavior is in her favor. Conflict is most likely to occur on those issues which are most heavily weighted by both parent and teen. Cooperation is most likely on issues which are heavily weighted by one partner and lightly weighted by the other.

Following the teen's behavior, the parent may supervise only two of the teen's six behaviors. Each time the teen is caught in a misbehavior, the parent may "punish" the teen by docking him up to 10 points. Also, each time the teen is caught misbehaving, the parent may supervise one additional issue.

The object of the game is to win as many points as possible. Players must learn to cooperate with each other in a competitive situation. Optimal strategy for both players in this mixed motive game would be shown by

(1) few issuances of orders; (2) low probability of disobedience; (3) low probability of punishment; (4) low amount (in points) of punishment (Stoll and McFarlane 1969: 263).

Research with GENERATION GAP

GENERATION GAP is played by only two players. Research with it shades into the area of *game theory* which is heavily social psychological (see Davis, 1983 or Auman, 1988, for a review of this literature).

Stoll and McFarlane (1969)

These investigators used data from thirty-three plays of GENERATION GAP in order to study the effects of same sex dyads and prior friendship between dyad partners upon consensus, disobedience, and punishment in the game. Results indicated that prior status characteristics of sex and friendship did influence play. Females and friends generally developed more consensus, and play involved few orders, less disobedience, and less punishment. Males tended to use coercion early in the game, and this strategy seemed to inhibit later formation of cooperation.

Parents in friendship dyads were less likely to punish, but when they did punish, they punished severely. This type of punishment proved to be more effective in forming a cooperative strategy. Stoll and McFarlane interpreted their results as follows:

> The expression of masculine role behavior mitigated against taking a cooperative stance in the game, even though the game highly rewarded cooperation. On the other hand, friends or females were able to respond consistently and more facilely within the player roles (Stoll and McFarlane, 1969: 268).

Boocock (1972)

Boocock used data produced by GENERATION GAP from seventeen parents and their real-life children in order to compare the results of play with reported actual behavior. Findings showed that strong relationships existed between issue weightings for both parents and teens during the game and their weightings on the same issues in real life. Parents and children were found to cope with controversial issues by avoiding completely communication about them.

THE COMMONS GAME

This simulation by Powers, Duus, and Norton (1980) draws upon the classic work of Hardin (1968) which has influenced social scientists from many disciplines. The logic of the commons relates to a number of computer modeling studies which predicted the collapse of the world system (representative works are: Barney, 1980; Mesarovic and Pestel, 1974; Meadows, Meadows, Randers, and Behrens, 1972). The *tragedy* of the Commons is that everyone has a short-term interest which favors exploitation of a common resource. The most frequent example is whales, but energy, minerals, farmland, and water are other examples of common resources. When everyone exploits them, in the long term the resource is used up, and no one benefits. The problem involves collective action to use the resource wisely.

The simulation can accommodate six to twenty players who compete for points. In each round of the game they secretly "play a card" which represents their action during the round regarding the pool of resources. Playing a red card represents responsible use of the resource (cooperation). It pays off modestly for the individual who plays it, and if all players opt for red, the pool increases. Playing a green card represents selfish exploitation of the resource pool (defection). It pays off much more handsomely for the individual than does playing red, but if many people play it, the pool diminishes, and all future plays of either red or green will pay off less. Playing a black card costs the individual, but it "fines" heavily everyone who played green (fining defection). It is similar to a police action. It is used to control "deviant" acts of selfish resource exploitation. Playing a yellow card earns a very small number of points no matter what others play and no matter how large or small the pool (independence). It is similar to bare subsistence. Finally, playing an orange card costs the individual who plays it, but it increases the value of any red card which is played by others in the game. It represents a bonus for the organized responsible use of the pool (rewarding cooperation). The resource pool in THE COMMONS GAME changes as a result of individual actions. If tragedy is to be averted, players must organize collectively to use the resources in a manner which is prudent.

Research with
THE COMMONS GAME

Since players must organize in order to take collective action in THE COMMONS GAME, its research strength is in the investigation of the effects of group characteristics and payoff structures on collective action. Studies by Powers and Boyle (1983) and Powers (1985) are examples of this type of research.

Powers and Boyle (1983)

The main independent variables of this study were: 1) whether players could play black (a penalty for defection) during a pretest run of the game, and partial versus complete information on how the resource pool worked. In the partial information condition, players were told how the payoff structure worked. In the complete information condition, players additionally were told that the pool was similar to harvesting fish in the ocean, i.e., taking points at a moderate rate would prevent the pool from being "fished-out." Also, players in the complete information condition were allowed to communicate with each other prior to play. The dependent variable of the study was the percentage of cooperative plays (red) versus defections (green) which occurred in a one-trial play of THE COMMONS GAME.

A total of 231 students competed with each other for class points in gaming groups having between six and ten players each. Players were randomly assigned to gaming groups, but the groups were not randomly assigned to treatments. The *fine* option (allowed to play black, i.e., to punish defection in the pre-test) resulted in significantly more cooperation (the playing of red) and in significantly less defection (the playing of green). Within the fine condition, the percentage of defection was significantly lower in the complete information condition than it was in the partial information condition. Both the fine option and complete information about the payoff structure significantly increased the amount of socially responsible behavior. In the *no-fine* condition, the percentage of cooperation (playing red) was significantly higher in the complete information condition.

Powers (1985)

The main independent variable of this study was the size of the group. Players participated in a fifty-trial commons game in either a six-person group or in a 15-18 person group. They played for points which contributed to their grade in an introductory psychology class. They were given an opportunity late in the course to take a chance on earning a greater number of points in an additional one-trial game or to withdraw from the commons and earn a modest number of points. The hypothesis to be tested was that as the size of the group increased from small to large, players would perceive a greater likelihood that other members of the group would exploit the pool, so players would choose to withdraw from the commons. Data from 510 players supported the theoretical model.

CONCLUSION

As an emerging research tradition, gamed simulation offers wide application for social scientists. Its major contribution has been the creation of different social worlds--worlds apart--in which the differences make a difference, i.e., they are meaningful in terms of theory.

Beyond the half-dozen games that were reviewed here, many more gamed simulations are potentially useful in this respect, and research with them offers a fruitful approach to greater understanding of social behavior.

CHAPTER THREE

THEORY

INTRODUCTION

The goal of this chapter is to integrate the divergent strands of theory that constitute an explanation of collective action in STARPOWER.

The levels of analysis are based on the work of Tilly (1978). Their time order matches that of STARPOWER. Briefly, the levels apply to the game as follows: social structure is created by the game rules. Players interact within the structure, and they form impressions of it. Next, social groups form. Then the groups interact with each other, and one of the groups changes the social structure through changes in the rules. Sometimes these changes in structure are a catalyst for collective action by the other group.

Brief Overview of Collective Action in STARPOWER

This research focuses on two sets of ideal-type simulated societies. In agrarian societies, status is based on ascription, and upward mobility is difficult if not impossible to achieve. In industrial societies, status is based on achievement, and mobility is less difficult. It is predicted that patterns of interaction, group organization, and change will differ between the two types of society. In the agrarian societies, ascription is likely to block individual action, so the groups become agents of conflict. In the industrial societies, individual action is more likely to result in mobility, so individuals remain in competition with each other.

SOCIAL STRUCTURE

Blau defines social structure as,

> the multidimensional space of social positions among which a population is distributed and which reflect and affect people's role relations and social association (Blau, 1977: 278).

His multidimensional space has two axes: inequality, a graduated parameter, and heterogeneity, a nominal parameter. A nominal parameter divides the population into subgroups with distinct boundaries. No inherent rank order exists among these subgroups in a society. Sex, religion, race and occupation are nominal parameters that are found in most societies. A graduated parameter differentiates people in terms of a rank order of status. Wealth, income, prestige, and authority are the graduated parameters that are found in most societies. STARPOWER is characterized by two graduated parameters (chip resources and income) and one nominal parameter (membership in the triangle or square group).

31

Blau uses the term "intersection" of parameters to mean that nominal parameters are independent of graduated parameters. He uses the term "consolidation" of parameters (similar to Landecker's *crystallization*, 1987: 40-43) to mean that they are related to each other. Consolidation of parameters means that membership in a certain group would predict high status. In the agrarian version of STARPOWER, assignment to the triangle or square group relates to both chip resources and income. If one is a square, chip resources and income are high. If one is a triangle, chip resources and income are low. The parameters are completely consolidated. In the industrial version of STARPOWER, assignment to the triangle or square group overlaps with chip resources, but it does not overlap with income. Through individual effort triangle players may earn high incomes and become squares in the game. The industrial version of STARPOWER is characterized by the intersection of group membership and income.

OPEN AND CLOSED SOCIAL SYSTEMS

Blau's concepts are linked closely to STARPOWER as well as to formulations of other theorists. The notion of open versus closed systems of stratification has been a central focus of Dahrendorf, Lenski, Van den Berghe, Durkheim, Marx, and Weber.

Dahrendorf

Two kinds of societies outlined by Dahrendorf were the capitalistic and industrial types. These types presented,

> The common factual skeleton of comparable societies without taking into account
> their cultural peculiarities (Dahrendorf, 1959: 40).

The concepts that he uses to describe how capitalistic societies evolve into industrial societies are separation of ownership and control, internal stratification, and increased mobility. In time each of these processes transforms the rigid homogenous classes of capitalistic societies into the heterogeneous groupings of pluralistic, industrial societies. In Blau's terms, consolidated parameters of capitalistic societies give way to intersecting parameters of industrial societies.

Lenski

This theorist used the level of technology in a society as the major explanation of distributive systems. Due to a higher level of technology, industrial societies are more productive than are the agrarian societies that they replaced. The distribution systems of industrial societies exhibit greater per capita income and lower inequality of both wealth and income. He writes,

> the appearance of the mature industrial societies marks the first significant reversal
> in the age-old evolutionary trend toward ever increasing inequality (Lenski, 1966:
> 308).

Van den Berghe

Van den Berghe (1967) outlined two types of social systems which he called paternalistic and competitive. Paternalistic systems are characterized by non-manufacturing economy, simple division of labor along racial lines (ascription), a large gap in living standards between castes, homogeneous upper caste, and a small dominant group. Competitive systems are characterized by large-scale industrial capitalism, complex division of labor organized around univeralistic criteria (achievement), narrower gaps in living standards between castes (between group homogeneity), greater gaps within castes (within group heterogeneity) and a large dominant group (Van den Berghe, 1967: 27-31). He claims that his distinction closely parallels that of Toinnes' *Gemeinschaft* and *Gesellschaft*. In Blau's terms, paternalistic social systems are characterized by almost complete overlap between a nominal parameter (race) and graduated status parameters such as wealth, income and educational level.

Durkheim

Durkheim conceptualized a continuum of societies from simple to complex based on their division of labor. The simplest society is one which has only one segment. The other end of the continuum is represented by a highly differentiated society. Two nodes on this continuum may be represented by the type of solidarity which is generated by the division of labor. These two types of solidarity are mechanical and organic. The basis of mechanical solidarity is a less developed division of labor in which the relationship between individuals is a result of resemblance or similitude (homogeneity). The structure of a society characterized by mechanical solidarity is said to be segmented. Its parts are not integrated in the sense of being complementary, rather the units are held together by a conscience collective, which is,

> The totality of beliefs and sentiments common to average citizens of the same society (Durkheim, 1933: 79).

The basis for organic solidarity is a well-developed division of labor in which the relationships among individuals are a result complementarity. The social structure is organized into a coherent whole through cooperation of the interrelated (not segmented) units. These units are more heterogeneous in nature, but they exhibit a greater interrelationship. In short, a well-developed division of labor is characterized by a greater degree of interdependence, while an undeveloped division of labor is characterized by less interdependence.

In the agrarian version of STARPOWER, chip resources are the most important determinants of wealth. For the upper class their possession does not depend upon other players in the game. In the industrial version, however, wealth is determined more by income which is earned through association with other players. The industrial version may be said to be characterized by greater interdependence among players than the agrarian version.

Marx

Marx argued that the economic basis of capitalism created a system of stratification which was characterized by two principal classes: the proletariat and the bourgeoisie. Each of these classes was composed of individuals who were similar to each other economically and different from members of the other class (Marx, 1956: Part 3). This notion implied that a large economic gap between the two classes was difficult to bridge, so the class system was characterized by low mobility (Marx, 1956: Part 3, V). Of course, Marx also envisioned a communistic, classless society of the future.

> The condition for the emancipation of the working class is the abolition of all classes . . . (Marx, 1956: 234).

This ideal future was characterized by a special type of homogeneity which is epitomized by the famous line,

> From each according to his ability, to each according to his needs (Marx, 1956: 258).

Both versions of STARPOWER are characterized by two social classes, but at least in the early rounds, the gaps between them are smaller and easier to bridge in the industrial than in the agrarian version. The closed system of stratification in the agrarian version is characterized by relative homogeneity within classes and heterogeneity between classes. The open system of stratification in the industrial version is characterized by relative heterogeneity within classes and homogeneity between them.

Weber

This theorist argued that societies were becoming more rational over time. Earlier societies (*Wertschaft*) were characterized by authority based on ingrained habituation (tradition). Later societies (*Gesellschaft*) were characterized by authority which was instrumentally rational (*Zweckrational*, see Weber, 1968). One of the ways in which organizations allocated individuals to roles in such a system (often referred to as rational-legal) was through their expertise rather than by criteria which had nothing to do with performance.

In a similar vein, Weber's discussion of "caste" (Gerth and Mills, 1946) involved the assignment of class and status position based on ethnicity, an assignment which was "less rational" than in the instance above. The typical way of describing the assignment of individuals to class position (and status position based upon ethnicity) was to say that an individual was ascribed these positions, while position in a rational legal organization was based upon an achieved characteristic of expertise. In Blau's terms, a caste system is characterized by the intersection of a nominal parameter (ethnic group) and graduated parameters of class and status. A class system is characterized by a certain amount of movement, or mobility, because position on graduated parameters is not tied to the more unchangeable nominal parameters. The closed system of stratification in the agrarian version of STARPOWER is characterized by ascribed status. In the open system of stratification, the industrial version of the game, status ascribed at the beginning of the game can be changed through achievement.

These theories provide links between analyses of actual societies and the characteristics of the simulated social structure that is created through play of the two versions of the gamed simulation. In the agrarian version, the graduated parameters of resources, income, and authority (authority is a dichotomy) are correlated (i.e., consolidated, Blau, 1977: 276) with each other and with the nominal parameter of square (upper-class) status. In the industrial version, the parameters of resources and group status are consolidated at the beginning of the game. Due to a high level of motility later on, the same persons do not occupy the social positions that they did at the beginning of the game, since in the industrial version trading has a great effect on income.

The industrial version exhibits more structural complexity than does the agrarian version. Structural complexity refers to

> the number of positions in multi-dimensional space and the distribution of people among them (Blau, 1977: 275).

This complexity is of a special type which should lead to a greater amount of association among all members of a social system. Put another way, this complexity should lead to a greater macrosocial integration (see below) of the simulated industrial societies.

IMPLICATIONS OF SOCIAL STRUCTURE
FOR EMPIRICAL PREDICTIONS
CONCERNING PLAY OF STARPOWER

The level of abstraction of Blau's theorizing allows it to subsume both the macro and micro levels of social analysis. As such, the theorizing is highly effective for the present attempt to use smaller groups in a simulated social system to represent larger groups of persons in non-simulated societies, i.e., entire social classes in the real world. Also, since Blau has contributed much systematization to the relations among social structure, status characteristics, and patterns of association, his theoretical scheme will be followed in this section. These relationships are summarized in Figure 3-1. A loose block-recursive scheme (see Blalock, 1969: 71-74) will be used to organize the discussion and subsequent analysis. The first block contains type and size of the simulated society and social class as predictors of status characteristics and patterns of association. The unit of analysis is the social class (and not the whole society), so the position of a class (upper versus lower) becomes important to this discussion. Figure 3-1 presents the basic blocks of the theoretical model and the interrelations among them.

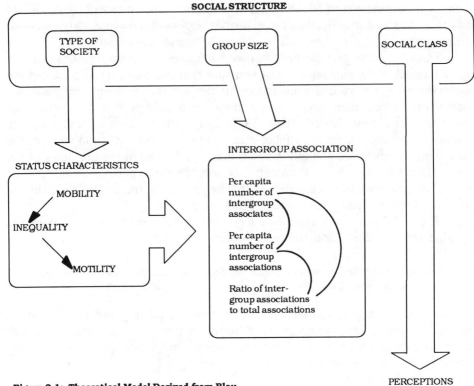

Figure 3-1: Theoretical Model Derived from Blau

In order to think of predictions in the conventional form of propositions, as presented by Zetterberg (1965), the two types of society may be thought of as nodes on a continuum of openness. For statistical purposes, the types will be treated as a dummy variable (see Kim and Kohout, 1975).

Societal Type

The first prediction is that the simulated industrial societies will be characterized by greater mobility (changes in wealth and income), within group inequality, and motility (changes in group membership; see below). Furthermore, mobility is predicted to affect inequality. Inequality is predicted to affect motility.

Group Size

Groups of different sizes also are represented within each type of simulated society. Group size is independent of type of society, and it is predicted to have an effect on the block in Figure 3-1 that is labeled "Intergroup Association." Blau places social association at the very center of his discourse on social relations. In his scheme, social association is the key to the integration of the parts of the social system. In fact, both "integration" and "discrimination" are defined in terms of associational patterns.

> Macrosocial integration refers to the extensive social associations among different groups . . . it is defined by the ratio of observed intergroup associations to those theoretically expected on the assumption of independence (Blau, 1977: 277).

> Discrimination . . . is the tendency of one group to restrict social intercourse with another (Blau, 1977: 276).

Blau also uses social association to transcend weaknesses in both social psychology and functionalism. This conception of macro-social integration,

> rests on the face-to-face associations between individuals from different groups and strata, not on their common values or sentiments, nor on the functional interdependence among different parts, though common values and interdependence may contribute to society's integration by fostering social intercourse between members of different groups and strata (Blau, 1977: 11).

The prediction of association from group size is as follows,

> The probability of association with many different persons increases with the increasing size and population density of the community (Blau, 1977: 181-2).

Size refers to the number of persons, and population density refers to the number of persons per unit of area. In STARPOWER, the area of the classroooms is a constant, so as size increases so does population density. Therefore, the greater the size of the simulated society, the greater should be the per capita number of associates. Furthermore,

> the probability of extensive intergroup relations increases as the size of groups distinguished by a given nominal parameter decreases (Blau, 1977: 42).

This proposition means that the smaller the group, the larger the per capita number of intergroup associations. Also, the smaller the group, the larger the ratio of intergroup to intragroup associations. Blau points out that small groups also are characterized by high ingroup cohesion, because the smaller the group, the greater the density of ingroup associations (see below). In STARPOWER, the density of both ingroup and outgroup associations varies together, since both groups are of equal size.

Density of association may be explained as follows: as size of the society increases, so does the number of players in one's own group. As the size of the society grows, so does the number of potential associates. The actual number of associates is influenced by factors other than size, so it does not grow at the same rate as the number of potential associates, given increases in size. Greater numbers of persons in a society tend to lower the ratio of actual associates to potential associates. Blau calls this ratio the density of group relations or group cohesion. This mechanism helps to explain why smaller groups tend to be more cohesive, but they also have more extensive out-group associations.

Social Class

Social class is independent of group size and type of society. It is predicted to influence interests and player perceptions more directly than any of the other components in the model. This relationship will be discussed in greater detail below.

STATUS CHARACTERISTICS

The graduated parameters of status characteristics include resources, earned income, investment income, and wealth.

Mobility

Social mobility refers to any change of status of the members of a group relative to the rest of the population (Blau, 1977: 277).

Intersecting parameters increase social mobility (Blau, 1977: 125).

Consolidated graduated parameters restrict vertical mobility (Blau, 1977: 125).

In the industrial version of STARPOWER the intersection of the graduated parameters results in higher mobility than in the agrarian version. To the extent that parameters intersect, upward mobility is both possible and probable (see also Berger, 1986: 58).

Inequality

Mobility along each of the parameters has an effect upon the degree of inequality in wealth (players' total scores). The mechanics of this relationship are discussed in great detail by Blau. Basically, he assumes that mobility will not be distributed evenly throughout members of a group, so it will increase the inequality among them (see also Turner, 1984: 203 and Berger, 1986: 46).

Motility

Blau uses the term "mobility" to refer to movement along a graduated parameter within a group. He uses the term "motility" to refer to changes in group membership. His usage is retained here. The amount of motility in a society is represented by the number of players who change groups. By the rules of the game, for each square who moves down to the triangle group, one triangle must move up to the square group.

The greater the inequality within groups, the greater the chances of highly mobile players in the triangle group earning more points than the less mobile members of the square group. If the triangle with the highest score has more points (wealth) than the square with the lowest score, then the players replace each other in the respective groups, i.e., motility. This procedure continues until the highest triangle has a score that is equal to, or lower than the lowest square; therefore, the greater the inequality within groups, the greater should be the motility. Motility has the effect of decreasing the inequality within groups, but it increases the inequality between groups. It lowers the status diversity within groups, and it raises the status diversity between groups. Mean status is raised for the square group, and it is lowered for the triangle group. In order to make this point in a different way, motility serves to reestablish the square-triangle boundary at the median of the distribution of wealth. Before motility, some triangles may have been wealthier than the median, and some squares may have been below median in wealth. Motility does not affect the inequality of the society as a whole, but it does raise the between-group inequality to the highest level possible given the particular distribution of scores and the requirement that the groups must remain equal in size.

Greater inequality within groups is predicted to result in greater association between groups; however, motility tends to raise the inequality between groups, so it is predicted to result in less association between groups. This effect may be blunted by the effect of having associates from previous rounds in the "other" group, a situation which would promote intergroup association for the motile players.

The discussion is not meant to imply that after motility, all simulated societies will have the same amount of within group and between group inequality. Overall, the simulated industrial societies will tend to have less between group inequality and more within-group inequality than will simulated agrarian societies.

For conceptual clarity, the distinction has been made between inequality within a group and the overall societal inequality, which is referred to as the inequality "between groups." Inequality within a group should raise the per capita number of intergroup associates, the per capita rate of intergroup association, and the ratio of intergroup associations to total associations. Inequality within a group can serve to raise motility (e.g. in the industrial version). Motility, as discussed above, tends to raise the inequality between groups, thus it lowers the indicators of intergroup association.

THE INTERGROUP
ASSOCIATION BLOCK

The prediction of increased intergroup association from increases in status characteristics (refer back to Figure 3-1) is based on the following theorems:

Social associations are more prevalent among persons in proximate than between those in distant social positions (Blau, 1977: 43).

Ingroup associations are more prevalent than outgroup associations (Blau, 1977: 43).

Social mobility promotes intergroup relations (Blau, 1977: 43, T-4).

High rates of mobility between groups promote high rates of association between their nonmobile as well as their mobile members (Blau, 1977: 43).

Mobility affects inequality, which in turn affects intergroup association (Blau, 1977: 43).

He points out that associations are based upon "common attributes" which people seek out or find rewarding in associates. Mobile persons retain some attributes in common with previous associates, and they continue to interact with previous associates. They acquire some new attributes in common with persons closer to their new status position, and they gain some new associates.

THE FORMATION OF INTERESTS
AND PERCEPTIONS

Tilly defines interests broadly enough to include perceptions. They are,

Gains and losses resulting from a group's interaction with [an]other group (Tilly, 1978:7).

To this definition, we might add the following phrase, "and the resulting more general human interpretations of the meaning of these interactions in terms of oneself, members of one's group, and members of other groups." This extension emphasizes the interpretations by individuals of what is happening to them.

Interests and Interest Groups

The central problem in defining interests is the distinction between objective interests resulting from one's position in the social structure and subjective interests as internal properties of individuals. Since the term has been used in both of these ways, Dahrendorf (1959) sought to clarify its usage. Objective or latent interests are conceptualized as a property of the social structure. They follow from the assumption that authority, a graduated parameter, is consolidated with class, so that,

differentially equipped authority positions in associations involve for their incumbents, conflicting interests. The occupants of positions of subjection hold, by virtue of these positions, certain interests which are contradictory in substance and direction (Dahrendorf, 1959: 173-174).

Those who share common latent interest positions do not constitute a group.

The aggregates of incumbents of positions with identical role interests are at best a potential group (Dahrendorf, 1959: 178).

He calls these aggregates quasi-groups. On the other hand,

> Interest groups are groups in the strict sense of the sociological term; and they are the real agents of group conflict. They have a structure, form of organization, a program or goal, and a personnel of members (Dahrendorf, 1959: 180).

Dahrendorf discusses three necessary conditions for interest group formation: technical conditions, political conditions, and social conditions.

Technical Conditions

Two major technical conditions are necessary for the formation of a manifest interest group. They are leadership and a program or charter.

> For an organized interest group to emerge from a quasi-group there have to be certain persons who make this organization their business, who carry it out practically and take the lead. Every party needs its founders (Dahrendorf, 1959: 185).

> While latent interests are nonpsychological orientations implicit in the social structure of roles and positions, manifest interests are articulate, formulated (or at least formulable) programs. They entail specific claims related to given structures of authority (Dahrendorf, 1959: 185-6).

In societies with open class systems interests imply individual strategies aimed at increasing wealth in order to maintain upper-class status for squares and to gain upper-class status for triangles. In societies with closed systems of stratification, interests are more apt to lead to a group orientation.

Political and Social Conditions

Dahrendorf identifies political and social conditions that are necessary for the formation of interest groups. They include political freedom to organize, communication between members, and patterned recruitment. The first of these elements, political freedom to organize, is constant across all plays of STARPOWER. Communication among members is close in meaning to Blau's social association. It should vary with the type of social structure and status characteristics, as predicted by the model. Recruitment of members is closest in meaning to motility in the Blau model.

Low motility groups maintain the same constituency over long periods of time, so recruitment should be easier. On the other hand, high motility brings group members together in a non-random way, so patterned recruitment also exists in highly motile societies as well. The amount of motility should affect the pattern of association within groups such that interests are more difficult to articulate. Groups with high motility rates, (i.e., those in industrial societies) should be more difficult to forge into interest groups.

A Model of Attitudes

Articulated interests are close in meaning to "attitudes" which have been a basic part of social science research for decades. Jones and Gerard (1967) have defined the term "attitude" in a way which identifies its source in a relatively clear fashion.

> an attitude is the result of combining a belief premise with a relevant value premise in a syllogism (Jones and Gerard, 1967: 707).

A belief is an assertion about "what is." It's an observation. It probably begins as an inkling, a feeling, at a preverbal level. Later, it becomes a perception, i.e., a working hypothesis which is revised as new information is added to existing stocks. Opinions of others are taken into account as the belief becomes more crystallized and is articulated at a verbal level.

A value is a judgment that at least implies what "should be." Useem's (1975) "organizing principles" have at their basis a blend of value and belief. Beliefs and values become linked to each other in a logically deductive manner, similar to a syllogism, in which belief and value are major premises, and the attitude is the result of deductive reasoning.

Relative Deprivation

Gurr proposed the concept of relative deprivation to link perceptions of fairness of the social structure to value judgments about one's situation within it. The result of deprivation is discontent, "a general spur to action" (Gurr, 1970: 24; see also Zimmermann, 1983: 31-36).

Efficacy and Mistrust

One of the most useful conceptualizations is that developed by Almond and Verba (1963: 196) and Gamson (1968). It involves the concepts of efficacy and mistrust as well as their statistical interaction. Almond and Verba argue that if an individual believes that he can exert influence on political decision makers (subjective political competence), he is more likely to try to use it. Stated in another way,

> The more subjectively competent an individual considers himself, the more likely he is to be politically active (Almond and Verba, 1963: 236).

Almond and Verba found that in the five countries which they studied, one-third of the respondents who were high on subjective competence reported actually having attempted political influence.

Gamson (1968) theorized that those individuals who are both mistrustful of those in positions of authority and who also have a sense of efficacy regarding their ability to influence incumbents, are most likely to mobilize and to engage in influence attempts.

> The efficacy dimension . . . refers to people's perception of their ability to influence;
> the [mis]trust dimension refers to their perception of the necessity for influence
> (Gamson, 1968: 42).

As presented by Gamson, efficacy and mistrust--when they occur together--should provide,

> the optimum combination for mobilization--a belief that influence is both possible
> and necessary (Gamson, 1968: 48).

Attitudes such as those of relative deprivation/discontent and efficacy and mistrust are a result of a more general and complex process. Willer (1967: 59-60) has codified this process to such an extent that even the theoretical concepts are defined in terms of one another, forming what he calls a "symbolic model." The Willer model provides a rationale for how social structure and interest groups are linked, but he omits discussion of intergroup association which would seem to play a strong part in linking social structure and attitudes.

Attitudes do not guarantee action, as shown by Willer and Zollschan (1964), Willer (1967), Wicker (1969), Deutcher (1973), Liska (1974), and Schuman and Johnson (1976). Even in instances in which action has a strong individual component, groups still play an important part in the attitude-behavior relationship (see Acock and DeFleur, 1972; Seidner and Dukes, 1976; Andrews and Kandel, 1979).

GROUP SIZE AND THE ORGANIZATION
OF INTEREST GROUPS

In collective action, of course, groups play the decisive part, and even if individuals have consensus on interests and attitudes, action is not guaranteed. No one has made this point made more poignantly than has Olson (1971). He argues that the link between common interests and group organization is problematic, and he reasons that even if collective action is necessary, individuals may try to remain uninvolved.

> Though all of the members of the group . . . have common interest in obtaining .
> . . collective benefit, they have no common interest in paying the cost of providing
> that collective good. Each would prefer that the others pay the entire cost, and
> ordinarily would get any benefit provided whether he had borne part of the cost or
> not (Olson, 1971: 21).

In the industrial version of STARPOWER, organization of an interest group would seem to present special difficulties as long as players could pursue individual strategies for upward mobility. Olson regarded the degree of openness of a social system as a constant, but he recognized that individual strategies were easier for persons to maintain in large versus small groups. Large groups can generate more power through their numbers, but they are more difficult to organize than are small ones. Members of a larger group feel that their own efforts may not affect any collective outcome and that their actions cannot be monitored by the group. Therefore, they feel free both to pursue an individual strategy and to try to share equally in any collective advantages which may come to the group. In smaller groups, individual members more clearly affect collective outcomes, and individual members can be singled out for special reward or punishment. Olson referred to these latter inducements as selective incentives. Olson's threshold in determining "large" groups is about twelve members. Group size in STARPOWER varies from five to eighteen members, so the data set contains some "large" groups.

Integration

In the previous sections, attitudes were conceptualized as a result of interaction with others within a social system. These attitudes could be the basis for social group formation. Furthermore, the type of society and the size of the group were seen as influences on the formation of an interest group. How does one know when it has formed and how well organized it is?

The notion of "togetherness" of a group is most closely related to the concept of cohesiveness, which in most literature is used to mean the attractiveness of the group for its members. Its inverse might be the de-identification with another group of which one is *not* a member. For instance, in STARPOWER triangle players may refuse to choose upward mobility if their own group is highly attractive to them. In actual practice, cohesiveness has not been a successful concept, so Dunphy (1972) has argued that the concept of group integration should be used in place of cohesiveness. Might integration signal the formation of an interest group?

Dunphy made a distinction between internal and external integration. Internal integration is based on commonness, similarity, and consensus among group members. This notion is consistent with the work of Durkheim, Blau, and others. Dunphy also discussed external integration which involves common orientations toward the other groups of which one is not a member. External integration includes autonomy which,

> refers to the amount of control members perceive themselves as possessing over issues significantly affecting group activities and group life (Dunphy, 1972: 275).

This concept is similar to efficacy of members within the group. Enclosure also is an important element of external integration. It is,

> the extent to which members are dependent on the group to pursue activities which they value (Dunphy, 1972: 276).

To the extent that players feel that they have control over issues affecting group activities, and to the extent that they feel dependent on their group to pursue individual activities, they will wish to remain group members and to use the group as a vehicle for attaining individual and group goals.

THE SECOND ROUND

In STARPOWER players may experience movement from one social class to another. After this motility, they know that wealth determines group membership, and they know that later in the game, group membership will be perfectly consolidated with authority. The groups are the decisive factor in the game. Especially in the agrarian version, the enactment of individual strategies by triangles most likely will be a frustrating and unsuccessful experience. In the industrial version, players can pursue individual strategies with relative ease and success.

Players most likely will enter the second bonus round with misgivings about members of the other group. Players have become active agents of their classes. Therefore, they are likely to view themselves and others as having internalized (or *manifested*) their interests. For all practical purposes the groups are in conflict with each other. The theoretical model for Round 2 which will be tested in Chapter Seven contains the same basic structure as the one presented earlier in Figure 3-1.

RULE CHANGE PORTION OF THE
GAME AND CLASS CONFLICT

At the time of the rule changes, class organization has been set up to distribute the chips, and perhaps the groups have skirmished with each other, but the full implications of the conflict situation that is generated by STARPOWER have not been realized by the players.

Even though simulated time accelerates many of the processes in STARPOWER, routinization of tasks within groups is not likely to take place. Organization of the groups, if it has occurred, most likely will have included the formation of a plan of action and the development of informal leadership. These conditions set the stage for collective action through fusion, Sartre's term for the rapid coming together of an action-taking group. Sartre's organized groups are similar to Dahrendorf/Willer's organized interest groups (Willer, 1967: 59), but Sartre's groups can take spontaneous action through fusion, but to do so they must mobilize.

MOBILIZATION

Gamson (1975) has detailed the problems of mobilization.

> Mobilization is a process of increasing the readiness to act collectively by building the loyalty of a constituency to an organization or to a group of leaders . . . mobilization is part of an organizing process that precedes specific efforts at influence (Gamson, 1975: 15).

In STARPOWER, a strong commitment to the group tends to offset the need for a complex role structure. Also, the individual player is not as limited by the group as she would be if the group became more organized, so internal conflict is less characteristic of groups in STARPOWER than would be the case if the game provided for a long lasting experience.

In the industrial version of STARPOWER, game rules serve to discourage early group organization in favor of individual action. Common interests are more difficult to discover. Group plans are more difficult to form. Leaders may achieve upward mobility to become members of the other group. The agrarian version of the game is characterized by more clearly delineated common group interests and stable groups (due to lower mobility). It seems to be a more likely setting for the organization of conflict groups than does the industrial version.

Leadership and
Plan of Action

Leadership involves the introduction of new ideas, and it helps to coordinate group activities. Typically, groups in STARPOWER will plan for everyone to "act together." Rarely do groups assign specialized tasks to their members. In this basic type of group organization, the centralization of authority is very important. Often it involves a single leader,

> a central figure around whom the organization revolves and with whom it is identified (Gamson, 1975: 93).

Only if the group solves both of its functional problems (of plan of action and leadership) will the group have achieved,

> the necessary combat readiness by marrying the willingness to obey and the right to command (Gamson, 1975: 90).

GROUP INTERACTION

Before a third round of the game is played, the upper class squares are given complete authority by the game director to change the rules. During this portion of the game, the interaction between the two groups becomes important. For instance, if the lower class demands rule changes, upper class members would be wise to regard this action as an indication of group organization, mobilization and a willingness to play within the rules (provided that some concessions are made). If the upper class fails to respond to lower class demands, subsequent lower class collective action may break existing rules.

The Bales (1950/1970) Interaction Process Analysis framework is comprised of four basic categories of emotion positive statements, neutral statements, questions, and statements that exhibit negative emotion. For interaction between two antagonistic groups, statements that are emotion positive represent acceptance of the other group, and interactions which show negative emotion represent rejection. Declarative statements tend to be cues to group organization and mobilization. Questions by members of the lower class can indicate lack of organization and acknowledgement of subordinate position. Questions by upper class members imply at least some acceptance of lower class members and their proposals. Unfortunately many upper class groups seriously underestimate the power of lower class groups. They tend to be insensitive to both the content and the process of these interactions and to the power relationships they belie.

RULE CHANGES

If an upper class receives complete authority to make rules, it is likely to create rules which favor it and repress the lower class. Discriminating rules which limit lower class rights (but do not limit those of the upper class) are a common form of repression. The lower class is likely to try to reduce its subjection to repression by refusing to play by repressive rules. Upper classes need lower class compliance in order to continue the society. Lower class mobilization threatens this compliance, so it changes the relative power positions of the two groups. Repression or failure to grant new opportunities to lower class members (especially in the agrarian version) threatens their already tenuous position, so if they are organized and mobilized, they may refuse to play by the rules, or they may refuse to play at all.

ELITE THEORY

Theorists such as Lundberg (1968), Mills (1956), and Domhoff (1967,1970) who subscribe to the Elite view of class relations predict that upper classes will attempt to further their own interests at the expense of other classes of society. Mills, in particular, emphasizes that upper class members use their positions of authority to make decisions which further their interests. Pluralist theory, as presented by Easton (1953) and others, also assumes that an elite will act in its own interest if it can, but as the issues change, so do the constituencies. Different coalitions form on each issue, so the same group of persons is not likely to win on all of them. At no time are actors expected to appear to be altruistic or generous unless it suits their purpose.

The industrial version of STARPOWER is characterized by the allocation of social position through achievement; thus it allows different players to become members of the upper class. In this way, the industrial version mirrors more of a pluralist conception of society, and the elite class is "abstract" (see Giddens, 1973: 120). On the other hand, the agrarian version provides for almost no mobility, so group membership is not likely to change. The same players have complete authority unless they decide to give it up--an unlikely occurrence from either perspective; thus, the agrarian version mirrors more of an elite view of society, i.e., the elite class is a "uniform" one (see Giddens, 1973: 120).

Both perspectives predict that as the elite becomes more organized and mobilized, it will become more efficient in pursuing its own interests. The game provides easy access to the rule-changing mechanism even for a relatively "abstract" elite group. Anyone can go up to the chalkboard and change the rules. Members of upper classes in simulated agrarian societies are predicted to make more frequent use of this rule-making authority in order to increase their trading advantages over members of the lower class. Of course, restrictive rules limit action which lower class members can take, so repression may encourage noncompliance. Also, the time required for implementation of a complicated set of rules by the upper class allows for further organization and mobilization of their opponents. Both Marx and Weber predicted an increase in domination by the upper class. For Marx, the upper class would become a ruling class, and for Weber, the society would become more rationalized, i.e., bureaucratized (see Offe, 1985: Chapter 10; Giddens, 1973: 125). Either way, an increase in legal norms will be a result.

LAW

Black (1976) has predicted that law will vary with characteristics of a social system. He defines law as, "the normative life of a state and its citizens such as legislation, litigation, and adjudication" (Black, 1976: 2). Law in society is mirrored in the game as the rules which are enacted by the upper class. Black presents a number of propositions concerning how the upper class is predicted to use the rules. He states that "law varies directly with stratification (Black, 1976: 13). The more the society is stratified, the greater will be the amount of law. Squares are predicted to use law to enhance their privileged position, and this use will be greater in the agrarian than in the industrial version.

Law, says Black, "varies directly with rank" (Black, 1976: 17), and lower ranks are predicted to have less law to protect them. When the law is analyzed for its protective value for persons of different social classes, lower classes are predicted to be protected less than upper classes, and this relationship will be more pronounced in agrarian societies than it will in industrial societies. Furthermore, from discussion in the preceding section, the most discrimination in law probably will occur when neither group is efficacious. Members of weak and inept upper classes are predicted to try to take advantage of their authority by making many discriminatory rules. This relation between weakness and discrimination should be more pronounced when the lower class shows itself to be weak and inept, i.e., it does not make credible demands, and when it does not threaten to take action on its own behalf.

The amount of law should vary inversely with the per capita number of associations between persons of different groups. Greater inequality between classes will result in more law to protect the elite. More law in an illegitimate system (an agrarian society) without elite coercive force (such as a weak upper class in STARPOWER) may be the wrong prescription for social order. In this situation, lower classes are predicted to engage in collective action against the upper class.

REPRESSION

Repression refers to lawmaking by the upper class that decreases mobility and motility opportunities for lower class members. Its opposite, facilitation, occurs when lawmaking increases these opportunities. Facilitation encourages lower class compliance, and it breaks down group-level mobilization into individual action (Tilly, 1978). Repression strengthens mobilization, and it encourages noncompliance. Therefore, the more repressive are the rules, the more likely should be the collective action. This relation may not be a linear one because, in industrial societies, the lower class can lose its opportunity for mobility, but in the agrarian societies, the lower class cannot lose what it never had.

COLLECTIVE ACTION

The game director gives complete authority to the upper class. They make the rules; however, in order to continue the society, compliance of the lower class is required. This requisite alters the power relations between the classes. Typically, lower class members are *told* what the new rules are and then they are *asked* to continue to participate in a more repressive society. If members of the lower class ever are going to protest collectively, their prime opportunity to act together occurs before anyone in their group can begin trading. The time is now! Sartre observes that the group may realize what has occurred and enter a state of fusion, i.e.,"the discovery of one's Self in the Other" (Hayim, 1980: 90). The group has not yet consolidated its internal structure. Group members have not undertaken any measures to preserve group unity (pledge), but the group can engage in purposive action (praxis) *as a group*. Fusion therefore asserts the humanness over mere objectivity. Individuals become third persons midway between seriality (a weak form of Durkheim's mechanical solidarity) and members of routinized groups.

> I see myself come to the group in him (Hayim, 1980: 91).

> This is the purest moment in human affiliation, the spontaneous moment of pure interiority which precedes all objectification by rules, rights, obligations, routines and so on (Hayim, 1980: 92).

> there is no Other, there are only several myselves (Sartre, 1976 as quoted in Hayim, 1980: 93).

According to Sartre, the group is fused. It is characterized by co-essentiality and co-responsibility which leads to an equalitarian character. Everyone is a leader.

The collective behavior tradition as developed by Smelser (1962) and by Turner and Killian (1972) accorded spontaneity a prominent place in its theoretical framework, but spontaneity was easily interpreted as a weakness in individual rationality. It was based on "losing oneself" in a group (Turner and Killian), and it could be based on incorrect information, e.g., a generalized (but untrue) belief (Smelser). Also, the collective behavior tradition ignored class conflicts and groups as agents of common interests. The groups were never really organized actors. They were *ad hoc* and unpredictable entities. The subsequent collective action tradition emphasized purposive action and rationality. It overlooked spontaneity, and disregarded its human component by taking the organized group as the unit of analysis (see Paige, 1971). On the other hand, collective behavior theory was more able to deal with individuals, group formation, and interaction. Collective action theory more adequately dealt with interaction between groups which had already formed and with longer term struggles between contender and incumbent groups. Analysis of STARPOWER requires a synthesis of the two traditions. Sartre ignores neither the group nor the individuals which make it up. Spontaneity is an affirmation of the human component of the fused group.

> The human world replaces, even if temporarily, the material world as the foundation
> of the group . . . The total group is identified not by an object lying beyond it, but
> by its self-oriented action (Hayim, 1980: 91).

Sartre does not abandon the purposive planning and leadership of conflict groups emphasized by collective action theorists, since fusion and consolidation can take place simultaneously. Complete consolidation of a group limits individual freedom, so spontaneous fusion becomes more difficult. Groups which are involved in protracted conflicts such as those studied by Gamson (1975) are less characterized by fusion in repeated confrontations than are the groups in STARPOWER. The fused state is more of a one-time resource of a group which must be replaced by more permanent forms of organization if the group is to continue to act.

THE RESULTS OF REPRESSION
AND COLLECTIVE ACTION

Most research on repression and collective action focuses on its determinants, not the results which follow from it. The action itself, of course, is more seductive than its aftermath; however, to overlook the results of collective action is to take a terribly myopic view of social relations. Conflict in the form of repression and collective action is likely to affect profoundly the subsequent relationships between the classes. Theory that was developed for earlier relations among classes predicts that the more repressive the new rules, the lower the status characteristics for lower class groups and the greater the upper class status characteristics relative to lower class status characteristics. Repressive rules mean that unless lower class players cheat, they will be at a disadvantage in Round 3. The theory predicts that the more severe the collective action, the less the intergroup association following it. More simply, classes will not trade with their enemies!

CHAPTER FOUR

HISTORY AND
RULES OF STARPOWER

HISTORY

The game was developed by R. Garry Shirts for a session on "race" at the National Council of Social Sciences. The first version was a role playing exercise. Its scenario portrayed an incident in a school cafeteria in which a food fight broke out between black and white students. The situation could not be handled by school authorities, so the police were called. The food fight quickly became a riot.

Participants in the exercise took the roles of white moderates, white extremists, black moderates, black extremists, and police. Their goal in the exercise was to determine what could be done about the problem that the riot revealed. A pretest was held on a college campus. It generated quite a reaction, as Shirts recalls,

> You must remember Stokely Carmichael and the various black leaders were making very inflammatory speeches at the time and the group that got the black militant role . . . stood up and started demanding their rights and yelling obscenities and having a great deal of fun portraying what they thought was the black militant extremist position. Everybody said they had had a great time (Coppard and Goodman, 1977: 493).

In spite of this apparent success, Shirts felt that the exercise was hardening stereotypes rather than breaking them up, so he started over. Shortly afterward, he saw an episode of the television series, *Startrek*. In the episode, Captain Kirk and the crew of Starship Enterprise met a character played by the impersonator/ actor Frank Gorshin who was white on the right side of his body and black on the left side. His nemesis was different in only one respect--his halves were reversed. He was black on the right and white on the left. Because of this difference the two characters were locked in a life and death struggle. It struck Shirts that the *Startrek* episode took place,

> . . . in a galaxy away from earth and as a result, [the writers were] able to deal with prejudice without the emotion and feeling that accompanies even the word "race" in our society (Coppard and Goodman, 1977: 494).

Perhaps the most important part of Gorshin's situation was that to the audience, the issue of "reversed colors" as a basis for the conflict seemed petty and irrational. Shirts began working with the notion that the purpose behind the game

51

should be hidden from players through abstraction, so he decided not to use the terms "race" or "black." Rather, he would build into the game the mechanisms of distinctiveness and privilege. He wanted to invite players to behave as did the combatants in the episode and then to have them become the audience so they could see the folly of meaningless distinctions and the arrogance of complete authority. The design came together while he was driving the car on a family trip to Palm Springs. As he tells the story, the children were making a racket in the back, and so to keep his composure he turned his thoughts to the game. During his time in the car, most of the recognizable features of the game came into being. The name STARPOWER paid homage to the source of Shirts' insight, and it kept the meaning of the exercise hidden from players, as he intended.

The materials for the first version of the game were Fisher Price toys that resembled a jumbo Tinkertoy™ building set. The nodes into which the dowel pieces fit came in three shapes--square, circle, and triangle. They were brightly colored three dimensional pieces about four inches in diameter. Colored yarn was slipped through the holes in the nodes so they could be worn about the neck. The toys created invidious distinctions among players that were just as ridiculous as those which had caused the struggle in the future galaxy. These toy artifacts became a central feature of the game because players attached value to them just as Gorshin and his nemesis did to their "halves" in the episode. In one early play, an upper class player ordered a triangle to give up a chip. The triangle asked him why. Taking off his node and shaking it in the triangle's face like a scepter, he thundered, "Because I'm a square!"

Shirts also knew that he wanted to structure the communication between players. At first players held the eight-inch dowel sticks that complemented the Fisher Price nodes. They were required to clasp these sticks together in order to begin talking. Younger players often hit each other on the head with the sticks instead of using them for their intended purpose, so the "stick rule" was replaced by a hand clasp rule in the current version.

Also, he wanted to create differences between the groups of players that would make them more culturally distinct but which would not really mean anything structurally in the game. Members of one group were required to talk with their tongues in their lips, and others had to be holding their ears. He describes it as "a pretty wild game." After several runs he realized that the "cultural differences" between the groups impeded communication and that the feelings of ingroup solidarity and outgroup hostility were plenty strong without them.

Shirts sent the game to a trusted friend who ran it at the conference. Play was quite lively as Shirts recalls,

> They had a near riot. They followed her around and chased her away. The Circles and Triangles took over, they kicked her out. It was very exciting. The game has been going very well ever since (Coppard and Goodman, 1977: 494).

At the time, Shirts was working for the Western Behavioral Sciences Institute, an organization in La Jolla, California that had three foci. The organization did quantitative research in social science. Also, it had a clinical focus due to the influence of Carl Rogers. Finally, it housed Project Simile, an undertaking that was funded by the Kettering Foundation and which included noted gamers, Wayman "Bud" Crow (founder of WBSI) and Hall Sprague. John Raser, author of *Simulation and Society* (1970), was on leave from WBSI during this time.

Project Simile had a broad mandate to explore simulation in education. Its charge included evaluation research of gamed simulations in learning. Also, it provided resources and support for teachers who already used games and simulations in their teaching. Part of this emphasis was the production of a newsletter on simulation in teaching that was published for seven years. A third emphasis of Project Simile was to actively recruit and train teachers as classroom gamers.

When funding ran out, Shirts started his own company, SIMILE II, to develop and market gamed simulations for education and to offer workshops on simulation for teachers and other professionals. STARPOWER first was offered from SIMILE II in 1969. It came as a complete game for up to 36 players or as a "do it yourself" instructor's manual. Due to the size of the "nodes," the package for the first one-hundred kits was a heavy wooden box the size of a file drawer.

In the second batch of kits, the nodes were replaced with flat pin-on badges, and the package was shrunk to a size little larger than a ream of paper. Shirts was worried. Since players attached so much meaning to the brightly colored nodes, would the game work as well without them? His concern was unnecessary, since there has never been an indication that the game lost any of its intensity due to the loss of resplendence.

STARPOWER was the first of nearly twenty successful gamed simulations to be developed and marketed by SIMILE II, including Shirts' personal favorite, BAFA' BAFA', a game in which "cultural differences" from STARPOWER came to fruition as the central feature in the creation of ethnocentrism. STARPOWER generated great interest during its first few years. Oddly, the enthusiasm had little to do with racial issues *per se*. The majority of sales were made to peace groups and to churches--and not to schools, as Shirts had expected. Players saw a striking parallel between the so-called "establishment" which favored the war in Viet Nam and citizens who opposed it. Without setting out to do so, Shirts had created a general model of class relations.

In 1974, the game was revised. In the earlier version of the game, players were assigned their class positions. These positions were difficult to change, similar to an agrarian society. Often players felt that this ascription did not represent modern society, so Shirts revised the game.

In the revised version, players who earned the highest scores in the first round were allowed to draw new chips from an "enriched bag" that contained many valuable ones. Players who earned lower scores in the first round were required to draw their chips from a bag that contained only those of lesser value. This revision by Shirts came after the establishment of the research methodology that is used in this book. The results are completely independent of each other, but they are almost exactly parallel solutions to the issue of "type of society" that has intrigued social scientists for over a century. Shirts' 1974 version of STARPOWER represented an industrial society, but it accomplished this task through the redistribution of resources rather than through trading. The agrarian and industrial versions of STARPOWER that appear in this volume were created by systematic variation of a bonus for the number of trades that are made by a player. The reader will note that STARPOWER as discussed in this volume contains only two social classes. These and other changes to the original STARPOWER procedures are discussed in Chapter Seven.

The 1974 version of STARPOWER retained all of the central features that had made it a classic. This second edition of STARPOWER has remained unchanged through the present time, and there are no plans to change it in the future. Interest in the game remained strong all through the 1970's making it the all time most widely played gamed simulation. In 1980 Shirts estimated that three to four million players had participated in STARPOWER. This estimate was quite conservative, since it was based on the assumption that fifty-percent of the kits actually were used and that twenty-five participants played each game.

In the 1980's STARPOWER regained the cult following that it had enjoyed during the Viet Nam era, but this time the stimulus for its popularity was closer to the racial situation that Shirts originally had intended to simulate. As the policy of apartheid in South Africa became a global political issue, players saw a striking similarity between Black South Africans and triangles in STARPOWER. Also, repressive rules that are made in desperation by squares in an attempt to stem the rising power of lower class members are seen as uncanny in their resemblance to the repressive policies of the White Afrikaners.

STARPOWER has been distributed internationally by the Oxfam organization as part of its program of assistance to developing nations. This dissemination--plus informal cultural diffusion--have made STARPOWER truly a world game. More than a few academic travelers have returned from remote areas with stories of the game being played with pebbles, bottle caps, or other readily available local artifacts. The meaning behind the badges has been extended beyond even that given to the original Fisher Price "nodes." The Masai of Africa reportedly use the bottle caps of premium beer for the square badges, and they use the caps from the least expensive beer as emblems of triangle status. Often the administrator of STARPOWER in one of these faroff places does not know the name of the game, and typically the rules have undergone distortions reminiscent of rumor, i.e., they changed incrementally each time they were transmitted orally. Despite some warpage in the rules, the notion of revolt is common to all versions of the game no matter how battered it has become as a result of its wanderings.

STARPOWER is considered by many gamers to have the dubious distinction of being "the all time most pirated game," depriving Shirts of his royalties. The game continues to have a strong presence in academic settings, and as a tool for inservice training it has become a part of the infrastructure of corporate life. Shirts has said that if he were beginning to market the game today, he would use the analogy of computer software rather than that of MONOPOLY. Thus, he would sell a license to use the game rather than selling the pieces and instructions outright, as one would sell a commodity. This system would produce income *over time* as opposed to the one-shot sale of a product. The issue of royalties is an important one, since supporting oneself on money that is generated through gamed simulations is almost an impossible task. Shirts has become a management consultant, and as of this writing he has spent the last seven years developing a training program for business and industry. Recently, he has returned to his first priority of gaming, and he is entertaining the notion of another company--maybe it will be called SIMILE IV--that would specialize in the development and marketing of a line of gamed simulations for business and industry.

There was a time when Shirts thought that a reasonably creative person was capable of producing scores of excellent gamed simulations. With hindsight, he now is concerned that painfully few really good ideas are produced even by the most creative people. Meanwhile, one of these seminal ideas, STARPOWER, has been played by 7-10 million players, and the end is nowhere in sight.

HOW STARPOWER IS PLAYED

A statement of the rules for STARPOWER can be found in the Director's Instructions to either of the two editions of the game. In the next section, a transcript of a play is provided. This transcript is written from the point of view of a player who has just completed the game. The transcript contains game rules and a script for the game administrator, but since it is intended to present the research procedures, someone who wants to administer the game will need the STARPOWER kit. Rules of STARPOWER that are cited in the transcript have been presented with permission from Shirts.

TRANSCRIPT OF A
PLAY OF STARPOWER

As players entered the classroom, they tried to find their usual seats among the two circles of chairs. Our guest, the game administrator, cautioned them, "Don't get too comfortable, because I am going to ask you to move to a different seat before our game begins." As students sat down, she gave each of them an envelope and said, "Don't let anyone see what is in your envelope." After most of the class had arrived, she introduced the game by saying, "The game we're going to play is called STARPOWER. It is a game of trading and bargaining for scarce resources in which the resources are colored chips of different values. These chips are traded with other players. The object of the game is to acquire the most points possible. The two players with the highest scores at the end of the game will be declared the winners.

"In your envelopes you will find white identification tags. Please pin them onto your clothing in a place where they *can* be seen easily by other players."

After players had pinned on their tags, she pointed to one set of chairs and said, "All right, let's have the squares sit here." Then she pointed to the other set of chairs and said, "Let's have the triangles sit here."

After everyone was seated, she said, "Also in your envelopes you should find five playing chips of different colors. Make sure that you have five chips." [What we didn't know was that squares received one yellow chip, one green one, and three random red, white, or blue chips. Triangles received five random red, white, or blue chips.] After all players had checked their chips, she pointed to the chalkboard. On it was written the information in Figure 4-1.

CHIP VALUES
Yellow = 80
Green = 25
Red = 15
White = 10
Blue = 5

COLOR BONUS
5 of a color = 25
4 of a color = 15
3 of a color = 10

TRADE BONUS
Each trade = 25

RULES
1. All chips must be hidden.

2. Players must hold hands to begin talking.

3. Players must keep holding hands until a trade has been made.

4. Trades must be one chip for one chip.

5. Chips of the same color cannot be traded for each other.

6. Players may avoid trading by folding their arms.

7. A majority vote by a group can expel a player from a group.

Figure 4-1: Rules for STARPOWER

Pointing to the chip values, she said, "If you have any yellow chips, they are worth eighty points each; greens are worth twenty-five points; reds are worth fifteen; whites are worth ten, and blues are worth five points each." Then she pointed to the color bonus and said, "In addition to the values of the chips you have, you will be given bonuses for having chips of the same color. "If you can get five of a color, you will receive an extra twenty-five points; four of a color are worth an extra fifteen points, and three of a color are worth an extra ten points. Don't compute your score now. We'll do that later. In a few minutes we are going to have a trading round. The round is about ten minutes long, and you will be allowed to trade with anyone in the room in an effort to maximize your points."

Then she pointed to the trade bonus and said, "In addition to the point values of your chips and the color bonus, you will receive twenty-five points each time you make a trade." [Later we learned that our game represented an industrial society. Had we been an agrarian society, we would have received only one bonus point per trade.]

Next she pointed to the rules and said, "Trades are governed by the following rules. First, all chips must be kept hidden. This rule will help you, since if another player sees that you have a valuable chip he may try to get it from you. Second, players must hold hands to begin talking, and players must keep holding hands until a trade has been made. All trades must be one chip for one chip. Trades of two for one or three for one are illegal. Chips of the same color cannot be traded for each other. A trade of a red for a red or a blue for a blue is illegal. A trade of a red for a blue is okay. If you do not wish to trade, simply fold your arms like this." She folded her arms pretzel-style. Then she said, "Finally, a majority vote can expel a player from a group. This rule will have more meaning later in the game."

She told us how to use the scoresheets. (See Appendix A.) She said, "In your envelope you will find a Player's Log. This log helps you keep track of your score, and it also helps us to understand the game after it's over. Take a look at your log. On the extreme right-hand side about a third of the way down the first page you will find an empty box. Please enter your tag number or letter in that box." She waited while we filled in our identification codes.

Then she said, "Now, just below the box in which you entered the number or letter on your identification tag you will find a row of boxes which are connected to each other. Each time you complete a trade with another player, write his or her tag number or letter in one of these boxes. This procedure automatically will keep track of the number of trades you make in the round. Do you have any questions?" A guy near the front of the room said that he was not sure how to trade. Without saying anything, the administrator beckoned to him to clasp her outstretched hand. When he did so, she said, "Now we can talk. Do you have any blues?" He shook his head, "Yes." She said, "I'll give you a white for a blue." He said, "Okay." Then she said, "That's all there is to it! Does anyone else have a question?" Several people hesitated as if they had questions, but she did not call on them. Instead she said, "The best way to learn about the game is to play it. You will have about ten minutes to improve your score. Remember you may get up, walk around, and trade with anyone in the room."

She set the timer. While we were trading she wrote the numbers of the squares on the chalkboard in one column, and she wrote the letters of the triangles on the board in a parallel column. Then the timer rang. She said, "That's the end of the trading round. Please return to your seats."

When everyone was seated, she told us how to compute our scores on the scoresheets. She said, "Total your score as follows: add up the values of the chips you have, and enter that number in the first box on the scoresheet below the ones in which you recorded the tag numbers or letters as you traded." Then she pointed to the chip values on the chalkboard and said, "Remember, yellows are worth eighty points apiece. Greens are worth twenty-five, reds are worth fifteen, whites are worth ten, and blues are worth five points each."

Then she pointed to the color bonus. "Next, give yourself the color bonus. Five chips of the same color are worth twenty-five points. Four identical chips are worth fifteen, and three of the same color are worth ten. Enter this number in the second box. Now, give yourself the twenty-five point bonus for each trade which you made during the round. You will know how many trades you have made by counting the number of boxes that you have filled-up on your scoresheet. Enter this number in the third box. Total those three numbers and give their sum to me when I call your tag number or letter." One by one she called out each number or letter from the chalkboard. She wrote down the score for each player next to the player's identification code.

After all of the scores were written on the chalkboard, she said, "Now we will have a group bonus round. Each group will receive three of these black chips." She held them up and said, "They are worth twenty points each. They will be added to the scores of players who receive them. Each group will have three minutes to come to a unanimous decision on who gets the chips. If a decision is not reached within three minutes--or if the decision is not unanimous--the game director will take back the chips, and no one will get them. More than one chip can be given to a player, but the chips cannot be split into fractions. They must be awarded as whole chips. They are not considered to have been properly allocated until players actually have taken possession of them.

At the end of the bonus round, any triangle who has a higher score than a square will trade places with him for the next round." She set the timer, and then she placed one stack of three chips on the floor in the center of square group. She placed the other stack of three chips on the floor in the middle of the triangle group. When the timer rang she looked at the members of the triangle group and asked, "Have you made your decision?" They said, "No, we're not quite finished." She said, "I'm sorry but I must take back the chips." Looking at the square group, she said, "Have you made your decision?" They said, "Yes." She said, "Is it unanimous?" They said, "Yes it is." She walked over to the chalkboard, and she asked them, "Which squares received the chips?" They told her, and she wrote the values next to their identification numbers. Then she said, "Players who received chips should enter their value in the fourth box on your scoresheets. Players who did not receive any chips should enter zero in the fourth box. Please return the black chips to me, as they cannot be traded, but you do get credit for them, since they already have been added to your score."

After the chips were collected she said, "Remember, if a triangle has a higher score than a square, they will trade places with each other for the next round. The way this procedure works is that we find the highest scoring triangle. Next we find the lowest scoring square, and we compare their scores. If the triangle has the higher score, the players switch tags and seats--but not envelopes--for the next round. If the square has the higher score--or if the scores are tied--the players do *not* switch tags and seats for the next round of play." We identified our highest triangle and our lowest square. The triangle's score was higher. She drew a line on the board that connected the tag number for the square with the tag letter of the triangle.

Then she explained, "Next, we need to find the highest *remaining* triangle and the lowest *remaining* square, and we compare their scores. If the triangle is higher in score, the players switch places. If the scores are tied, or if the square has the higher score, then the players do not switch places." We repeated this process a few times until the score of the lowest square was higher than that of the highest triangle. The game administrator said, "Now we will switch tags and seats for the next round, but everyone will keep his or her envelope. If your tag number or letter is connected by a chalkline to that of another player, find him or her and switch tags and envelopes."

After players had switched places, she told us, "Please turn your player's logs to the second page and answer the questions on the sheet. The term 'group' in the questions refers to the group in which you now are sitting." After we finished answering the questions, she said, "Please turn your log to the third page. Enter your current tag number or letter in the appropriate box just as you did in the first round." After we had completed the entry, she said, "Now we will have a second trading round which is exactly like the first one. After the trading round we'll have another group bonus round, but after players exchange places, the squares will be given the authority to make rules for a third round of play. You will have about ten minutes to improve your score." She set the timer.

While we were trading, the game administrator erased the first round scores from the chalkboard. She left the tag identification numbers and letters as they were. When the timer rang she announced, "That's the end of the trading round. Please return to your seats. Total your score for this round in exactly the same way as for the first round--with one exception: in the first box you are to enter your total score from the first round. In the second box, enter the values of the chips you now have. In the third box, enter the bonus for chips of the same color. In the fourth box, enter the bonus for the number of trades. Add up the four boxes and give me your score when I call out your tag number or letter."

When all of the scores had been tallied on the chalkboard, she said, "Now we will have a group bonus round exactly like the last one. Then any triangle with a higher score than that of a square again will change places with him for the next round. But, as I said earlier, before we have the third round, the game rules say that the group that has worked the hardest will be given the chance to make any rule changes it wishes for the third round." We did the bonus round just like before, but this time both groups allocated the bonus chips successfully. Two pairs of players changed groups. Next we completed some questions on our scoresheet. There were more of them than in the first round.

When we were finished answering the questions, the game administrator said, "As I mentioned before, since the squares have worked the hardest, as shown by their scores, they will have the authority to make changes in the rules for the third round. Triangles may suggest rules, but the squares have the authority to implement them. Changes must be recorded on the chalkboard by erasing a rule and/or writing a new one, so we may see the rules by which we are to play." After she said this, she placed a piece of chalk and an eraser on the floor in the center of the square group. Then she walked to the rear of the classroom and sat down. One of the triangles asked her, "How long will the third round be?" She replied, "Squares make the rules." Then a square asked, "Can we change Rule 2?" The game administrator stated, "You make the rules." The squares got rid of the first five rules, and then they asked the game administrator to set the timer for five minutes. She did so.

Almost everyone began trading a lot. After the timer rang, she said, "Please total your scores like before, and give them to me when I call your tag number or letter." She erased the scores from the second round, and then she began calling out the tag numbers. After all scores were tallied on the chalkboard she said, "We will not have a group bonus session, but let's see which players would be likely to change places if we continued the game." We compared the highest triangle with the lowest square. We continued this process as in the earlier rounds. Two pairs of players would have changed places if we had continued the game.

Next, the game administrator told us, "Please answer the final page of questions on your scoresheet. The term 'group' refers to the group in which you now are sitting." After we answered the questions, she said, "Please put everything back into your envelope. Do not forget to take off your identification tags." After the materials had been put back into the envelopes, she said, "Please hand in your envelopes, and please move the chairs back into their usual places, and we will talk about the game."

When we had returned to our usual places in the classroom, the game administrator asked, "Well, what happened in the game?" Players talked about the trades that they had made, and the triangles complained that the squares had erased five rules without consulting them, but nevertheless two triangles had become squares, just like in the second round. The game had proceeded in the third round with "business as usual." She explained that the behaviors of players are influenced heavily by their position in the social structure of the game, so we should not be too quick to "blame" another player personally for actions that we felt were capricious or malevolent. She said that squares almost always make at least a few rules that repress triangles. In fact, triangles expect the squares to do so!

Next, the game administrator said, "The game is like a poem, a novel, or a work of art. It contains many meanings which we can analyze. Some of these meanings may not have been intended by the author. STARPOWER is rich in these possible interpretations. That is why it is such a good learning device. After observing many plays, here's what I see. The chips represent resources in their most general sense. Yellow and green chips are very valuable by themselves. Their inherent worth goes beyond their combination with other chips. These chips truly are scarce resources such as water in the desert, food during a famine, or gold during a time of monetary panic.

"Some chips, like blue ones, can double their face value in combination with each other. The color bonus represents the excess value of having more of something. If I have a few acres of land, I can feed my family through farming. If I have more land, I can realize a profit by selling my crops. Most players earn one of the color bonuses at some time during the game.

"If you were a square, you began the game with one yellow chip, one green, and three random red, white or blue chips. If you were a triangle, you began with five random red, white, or blue chips. Squares started with approximately 139 points on the average, and triangles began with approximately fifty-seven points.

"The first rule states that, 'All chips must be hidden.' Outside of the game, usually we do not know someone's resources exactly. We may have a rough idea from their clothes, job, house or other indicator that is similar to the square or triangular badge worn in the game, but we never know exactly. How does this rule protect those with valuable chips? That's right, if someone knew what you had, he might keep holding your hand to try to force you to give it up. Bank accounts are secret just like those chips.

"The second rule states that, 'Players must hold hands to begin talking.' Hand-holding symbolizes formal entry into a social exchange relationship. We have procedures similar to it in other aspects of social life: a handshake to consummate an agreement, signing on the dotted line, stepping across the line for entry into the military, or even saying, 'I do' in the marriage ceremony. Once we're in the relationship, we have rules which govern it. Often, the implications of the rules which will bind us in the exchange relationships are not fully known to us at entry. Many rules are written in 'fine print.'

"The third rule states that, 'Players must keep holding hands until a trade has been made.' We have rules for ending an exchange relationship too. These rules usually specify a penalty to be paid by the partner who 'wants out' early, late, or under conditions which are different from those at entry. Just as we may be involved in late penalties, pre-payment penalties, or even divorce settlements, in the game the player who is most anxious to break-off the trade may have to give up a valuable chip.

"The fourth and fifth rules state that, 'Trades must be one chip for one chip,' and 'Chips of the same color cannot be traded for each other.' In effect, Garry Shirts, the game designer, is saying that almost all exchanges in society are unequal. Someone almost always wins, and someone almost always loses in every exchange, if only by a small amount. Exactly even exchanges are quite rare. When we come home from shopping, our 'bargains' are uneven exchanges in which we feel that we've won. Often, our exchanges are informal and they do not involve money. Peter Blau, a sociologist, studied how supervisors may exchange needed information to subordinates for personal compliments.

"Rule 6 states that, 'Players may avoid trading by folding their arms.' The game permits players to 'stand pat' or to 'drop out.' It allows players to avoid trading if they want to.

"Rule 7 states that, 'A majority vote by a group can expel a player from that group.' This rule means that the other players can kick you out of the group. What if a player threatens his group by asserting that if they don't give him a bonus chip, he'll not agree to be unanimous, so the group will lose the bonus chips? What will they do? That's right! They'll kick him out!

"What will the squares do if a former triangle tries too hard to influence them to make rules that are beneficial to the triangles? That's right! They'll send him back.

"In your society each time you made a trade, you received a bonus of twenty-five points. That means that if you were a triangle, you had a good chance of becoming a square by making lots of trades. This process is called achieved status, and it is characteristic of more technologically advanced societies in which each unit of work (each trade) pays off highly for each player. In this society, if an average triangle makes four more trades than an average square, he can become a member of the square group. Sometimes we play the game under a set of rules that gives a bonus of only one point for each trade. This process is called ascribed status. It can be very difficult to get ahead if your ascribed status means that you are not allowed to participate fully in the society. Ascribed status is characteristic of agrarian, or pre-industrial, societies.

"If you are a square in an agrarian society, what's your best strategy? That's right, hang onto your yellow chip. That's all you have to do. What if you're a square in an industrial society? You better make as many trades as possible.

"Is our society characterized more by achievement or ascription? Like most industrial societies, our society has a strong emphasis on achievement, but some ascribed statuses still persist. For instance, if you're 'too young,' 'too old,' female, or non-white, it is more difficult to get ahead, so we still have ascription. No real society is a perfect example of either achieved or ascribed statuses, but STARPOWER can simulate perfect achievement or ascription, so the game can help us learn how real societies might work.

"Do groups or individuals win in STARPOWER? What about in actual society? That's right, it is not really clear. In the industrial version individuals have a bigger role, and in the agrarian version, groups are more important. But just like real society, it is not clear whether we compete as groups or as individuals. Gamers call it a 'mixed-motive' situation.

"Sometimes, the squares make rules that are just awful, and sometimes the triangles revolt against them. Why do you think that happens? That's right, in agrarian societies the triangles may feel that they can't win no matter what they do. Incidentally, it is very rare for industrial societies in the real world have a revolution. It is much more common for agrarian societies to have them. Usually, the triangles are rural people, and the squares are urban. Marx thought that the revolutionaries would be factory workers, but they turned out to be peasants. The workers formed unions to help them get ahead, but peasants generally did not, so things did not improve for them.

"One final point. In most societies investment occurs. Scores are carried forward from previous rounds to later ones. Advantages from earlier rounds are increased in later ones, so mobility can become even more difficult in later rounds. Can you give some examples of this process? What would it be like to be a serf in a feudal system? How did the 'robber-barons' found family dynasties in the United States?"

The students gave some really good answers to these questions, and then the time for our class ran out. Students appeared to have enjoyed the game, but nobody in our game *liked* being a triangle!

CHAPTER FIVE

OPERATIONALIZATION OF CONCEPTS
OF THE THEORY MODEL

In Chapter Three, a theory model was developed to explain collective action in STARPOWER. In this chapter, the concepts of the model will be provided with operational definitions. These operationalizations are intended to make sense in the real world and in the "world apart" of the STARPOWER simulation.

THE SOCIAL STRUCTURAL BLOCK:
MANIPULATED VARIABLES

The first block of the Blau Model discussed in Chapter Three includes three variables: 1) the type of society (agrarian or industrial), 2) the position of the social class (lower or upper), and 3) the size of the social class (five to eighteen members). These variables were manipulated in an experimental design (see Chapter Seven), so some explanation seems warranted here. Game groups were randomly assigned to either the agrarian or the industrial version of STARPOWER. In the industrial version of the game, each trade which a player completed was worth twenty-five points. In the agrarian version of the game, each trade was worth only one point. The tremendous implications of type of society were discussed in Chapter Three. Within game groups, players were randomly assigned either to the upper or to the lower class. The classes were formed by the assignment of a single yellow chip, a single green chip, and three randomly chosen red, white, or blue chips to each upper class player (139 points average), and five randomly chosen red, white, or blue chips were assigned to each lower class player (fifty-seven points average). Members of the classes were identified by badges that were made in the shape of squares (upper) or triangles (lower). Squares sat in one part of the classroom, and the triangles sat in another part. Groups of equal size were matched across the agrarian and industrial versions of the game, and the social classes were of the same size (see Chapter Seven).

The type of social system (agrarian or industrial) and the position of the social class (lower or upper) represented dichotomous (dummy) variables. The number of players in a social class was a ratio scale. A total of 128 social classes made up the data set: thirty-two upper classes and thirty-two lower classes participated in the agrarian version of STARPOWER, and thirty-two upper classes and thirty-two lower classes participated in the industrial version.

VARIABLES OF THE STATUS
CHARACTERISTICS BLOCK
Mobility

The status characteristics block (see Figure 3-1) is made up of the three variables of mobility, inequality and motility. The first of these variables, social mobility, is defined by Blau as,

> any change of status of the members of a stratum or group relative to the rest of the population (Blau, 1977: 277).

For this research, changes in wealth (i.e., the total score of a group) were used as the operational definition of mobility. Mobility in the first round was measured by subtracting a group's average score at the end of the round from the average group score in the beginning of the game (fifty-seven points per player for lower class triangles and 139 points per player for upper class squares). For later rounds of the game, mobility for a group was determined by subtracting the average score for a group in the previous round from the average score for that group in the subsequent round.

Inequality

An index of inequality is a measure of the dispersion of scores, and several specialized measures of inequality are available. Allison (1978) reviews a number of these indices, including the Gini index, Theil's measure, and the coefficient of variation. He concludes that Theil's measure is the best one for data such as those in STARPOWER.

> Because its sensitivity to transfers decreases as scores increase, Theil's measure is especially desirable for measuring inequality of income, or other social rewards having diminishing marginal utility (Allison, 1978: 877).

Distinctions among the measures of inequality are not critical when the primary method of analysis is the correlation coefficient, as is the case in this research. Allison demonstrates how all of the measures are special cases of the variance of the log normal distribution of scores after each score is transformed into its natural logarithm. Each of the three measures of inequality represents a linear transformation of the variance of the logged scores. As such, correlations between any of these measures and another variable will be equal. The index of inequality used in this research, Theil's Index, is the variance of the log normal distribution of wealth owned by a group.

Motility

At the end of each round of the game, some players may change social classes. In STARPOWER, motility divides players into two social classes at the median of the distribution of game scores, i.e., by wealth. The process is one which Blau refers to as motility, which is,

Mobility of equal numbers between groups or strata in both directions, which leaves the distribution among positions unaltered (Blau, 1977: 277).

Let us review the mobility procedure. Players are told that if the highest scoring triangle has a higher score than the lowest scoring square, then the two players will trade seats and identification tags for the subsequent round. The triangle will be upwardly motile, and the square will be downwardly motile. Next, the highest scoring player remaining among the triangles is compared with the lowest scoring square. If the triangle's score is higher, the players switch. This process is continued until the lowest square's score is equal to--or higher than--that of the triangle. (For more information on this process, see Chapter Four.) The variable of motility has zero as its lowest value (no player moved to the other social class), and it cannot exceed the number of players in a social class (every player in one social class moved to the other one).

The Status Characteristics Block

The block of variables called status characteristics was created by combining mobility (changes in wealth of a social class), inequality (variation in wealth within a social class), and motility (changes in social class membership). In order to combine the variables, each of them was put into standard score form. The variables then were added to each other to form the block. Social structural variables were used to predict this block, and in turn this block of status characteristics was used to predict the next one, that of intergroup association.

Intergroup Association

The concept of association is operationally defined as a trade during the game. A record of trades is kept on each player's scoresheet (see Appendix A). In order for a player to get credit for a trade, she must write down the badge number or letter of the person with whom she traded. After the game was over, the researcher counted the number of trades which each player had completed with members of her own group and with members of the other group. For example, if player "AB" (a lower class triangle) made five trades with other players having lettered identification tags (other triangles), five ingroup trades would be recorded. If this player also made four trades with players having numbered identification tags (upper class squares), four outgroup trades would be recorded.

For this research, three ratio-scale measures of intergroup association proposed by Blau (1977) were computed. First, the *per capita number of intergroup associates* was computed by counting the number of different outgroup players with which each player in a group made at least one trade during a round of the game. These totals were summed over all players in the group. The sum was divided by the number of players in the group. The minimum value of the variable was zero (no trades were made by any member of a social class with any member of the other social class). The maximum value of the variable was equal to the number of players in the other social class. This maximum value would be reached only if every member of one social class made at least one trade with every member of the other social class.

The *per capita number of intergroup associations* was computed by counting the total number of trades made by players in a group with members of the outgroup. The total was divided by the number of players in the group. This variable had a minimum value of zero. Its maximum value was limited by the number of trades which players could complete during the ten-minute trading round.

The *ratio of intergroup associations to total associations* was computed by dividing the number of outgroup trades by the total number of trades (ingroup plus outgroup) made by a group during a trading round. This variable had a minimum value of zero (no trades with members of the other social class) and a maximum value of one (trades were made exclusively with members of the other social class).

Since each of these three variables is a slightly different measure of the extent of intergroup association, they are predicted to be interrelated with each other, but this interrelation is not assumed to be causal. In order to form the block of Intergroup Association, each of the three measures was converted into a standard score. These scores were added to each other to obtain the value for the block.

Group Organization
And Group Action

The first indication of emerging group organization that could be observed in the game was the successful allocation of the three group bonus chips to group members. In order for this allocation to be successful, the group must have reached a unanimous decision on which players were to receive chips. Furthermore, this decision must have been made within a three-minute time limit. Also, the chips must have been picked up from the floor of the classroom, and possession of the chips must have been taken by their legitimate recipients. If any of these conditions did not hold, the game administrator took back the chips, and no one in the group received any of them. The successful or unsuccessful allocation (coded "1" or "0") of these chips was recorded on the scoresheets by players.

Perceptions

At the end of Round 1, players were asked two questions about their experiences in the game. They were asked about their desires for individual motility and their perceptions of openness of the social structure. In order to measure their desires for motility, players were asked about the extent to which they agreed/disagreed on a five-point response scale with the Likert-type item which stated, "If I had a chance I would like to become a member of the other group." In order to measure a player's perception of openness, he was asked the extent to which he agreed/disagreed with the statement, "A triangle can become a square if he really tries." Individual answers were scaled 1 (strongly disagree) to 5 (strongly agree), and these answers were aggregated for each social class in the game. Since there was no strong theoretical rationale for combining them, and since the two components were not correlated ($r = .06$), they were treated separately in the analysis.

ROUND 2

The operational definitions for the variables from the first round, social structure, status characteristics, intergroup association, and group action, remain unchanged in Round 2.

The sequence of activities for players in the second round was identical to that of the first. The activities were as follows: 1) trading period, 2) computation and reportage of scores, 3) group bonus and the addition of group bonus points to scores, 4) motility, and 5) completion of questionnaire items on perceptions.

During the instructions to players for the group bonus portion of Round 2, the idea was made clear to players that upper class members would make the game rules for the third round of STARPOWER. Immediately after the changes in group membership occurred, players were asked to complete about a dozen questionnaire items on their perceptions and attitudes concerning the game. Most of these questions were not asked after Round 1, because at that time players were just beginning to learn about the game. By the end of Round 2 they became much more familiar with the rules. They had a better idea of how the social structure and the class system worked, and they had time to discuss these characteristics of the game with other players. The items asked players their views about their own group as well as those of the other group. Data were gathered from individuals, and then they were aggregated for the group. The items are presented in Appendix A.

Rules in the Best Interests
Of Our Group

At the end of Round 1, players were asked about their desires for motility and their perceptions of openness. After Round 2, in addition to these two questions, players also were asked about their perceptions of the game rules in relation to their social class positions with a Likert-type item which said,

"The game rules are in the best interests of our group."

A five-point response scale measured the amount of agreement-disagreement with the item. Individual responses were averaged for the group.

Efficacy

Individual efficacy was measured by aggregating for each group the scores on agreement/disagreement with the following Likert-type item:

"Players like me don't have any say about what the other group does."

Thanks to an anonymous reviewer for a social science journal, a measure of group efficacy also was incorporated into the questionnaire for the latter half of the plays. It read:

"Even if players like us act together, we can't have much effect on what the other group does."

The two measures of efficacy correlated .57. While this association is far from perfect, either one of the two measures of efficacy predicted subsequent variables in the model equally well. During the data analysis a decision was made to eliminate group efficacy from it, due to so much missing data.

Mistrust

The variable of mistrust was measured by a Likert-type item which stated,

"The other group can't be trusted to do what is right."

Scores for individuals were aggregated for each group on the extent of agreement/disagreement with this item.

Deprivation

Several measures of deprivation have been identified by theorists as preconditions of collective action. In this research two measures of deprivation were considered.

Absolute deprivation for a group was measured by using the aggregate average of answers to the question:

"How would you describe *your present* situation in the game?

Best possible __ __ __ __ __ __ __ worst possible"

Perceived deprivation of the other group was measured by using the group average of answers to the question:

"How would you describe the present situation of the other group?"

Best possible __ __ __ __ __ __ __ worst possible"

Relative deprivation was measured by taking the *difference between* the answers to these two questions. Despite the arguments on the theoretical level (see Gurr, 1970) of the importance of relative versus absolute deprivation, the data from STARPOWER show these two variables to be highly intercorrelated (r = .91), so they were added together to form a block called "deprivation."

Group Organization

Two major aspects of group organization which emerged from the theoretical analysis were the development of a set of roles within the group, the most important of which was that of a leader, and the development of a plan of action. The measures of leadership and plans of action were based on perceptions of players. For the sake of clarity these two components of group organization were analyzed separately.

Leadership

The variable of consensus on leadership was measured by tabulating answers to the following item,

> "Who is the player who has done the most to help your group move toward its goals?
> ____ (Enter his tag number or letter here)"

Various components of measures of leadership were derived from answers to this question. For each group the following information was recorded: 1) the number of "votes" received by the player who received the most votes in a group, 2) the number of votes received by the person receiving the second-highest number of votes in the group, 3) the number of players who did not answer the question, and 4) the number of players in the group. Several measures of leadership were derived from these components. Empirically, the strongest measure of leadership was the number of votes received by the most highly cited player divided by the number of persons in the group.

Plan of Action

In order to measure the extent to which groups perceived themselves to have developed a plan of action, players responded to the following Likert-type item,

> "Our group operates with sets of conflicting plans."

Individual scores on agreement/disagreement with this assertion were aggregated at the group level. This variable was re-scaled so that the highest numerical values represented the *least* conflict in plans, i.e., the most organization. Test-retest reliability coefficients (using Robinson's A) ranged from .88 to .96 for the measures of perceptions and attitudes that were discussed in this section.

THE RULE CHANGE
PORTION OF THE GAME

During this portion of STARPOWER, the members of both classes were reminded that the upper class members had the authority to change the game rules for the third round. Both classes were told that the lower class triangles could suggest possible rule changes, but the upper class squares actually had the authority to implement changes.

The main dependent variables to be considered in this section included the number of rule changes made by upper class members and the repressiveness of new rules. Predictor variables available for the analysis included characteristics of social structure (such as society type and group size) and perceptions of play (such as efficacy, mistrust, leadership, and plan of action). For a more complete discussion of the predicted relations among these variables, see Chapter Six.

For the first time in the game, the two classes which made up each society had functional differences in the form of complete rule making authority of the upper class versus no authority for the lower class. The units of analysis became the sixty-four societies. In the previous sections, the 128 social classes had been the units of analysis.

Measures

At the beginning of the rule-change portion of the game a piece of chalk and an eraser were placed in the middle of the square group by the game administrator. Players were told that all rule changes must be recorded on the chalkboard for all players to see. Any time a rule was changed, the observer recorded the change in a notebook (see Chapter Seven). The addition of a new rule to the game constituted a change, as did the erasure of an existing rule. If an existing rule was modified by a square player, the occurrence was recorded as a single change. By this procedure, erasure of an existing rule and the addition of a new rule which took its place constituted two rule changes. All changes were summed for each game play.

Repressiveness

Repressiveness of rule changes was measured by scoring each rule change on its implications for later play of the game. The categories of this scale are presented in Figure 5-1. Rules which singled out a class for privilege or repression (particularistic rules) were scored further from the middle of the index than rules which did not single out a particular class (universalistic rules). Within the universalistic rules, a distinction was made between overt and covert repression. The implications of overt repression were easily identified as benefiting (or repressing) one of the classes. Covert rules were judged to be more subtle in their effect. The coding of a rule change took into account whether the society was of the agrarian or the industrial type. For example in an industrial society, raising the value of yellow chips was considered to be a covert benefit, because by the third round not all of the upper class members had a yellow chip.

Code	Effect of Rule	Example
12	Upper class ends game (state or imply that upper class won the game)	"We won"
11	Particularistic, differentially applied rule which prevents mobility	"Triangles cannot become squares"
10	Particularistic, differentially applied rule which limits exchanges to the upper class or among the lower class	"Triangles can trade only with squares"
9	Particularistic, differentially applied rule which creates disadvantages for triangles and advantages for squares in exchanges	"Triangles must show chips to squares"
8	Universalistic rule which overtly favors upper class members	Raising the value of yellow chips (esp. agrarian version)
7	Universalistic rule which covertly favors upper class members	Elimination of Rule 2: "Players must keep holding hands until a trade has been made."
6	Universalistic neutral rule	
5	Universalistic rule which covertly favors class members	Raising value of red chips (esp. agrarian version)
4	Universalistic rule which favors lower class members	Equalizing all points
3	Particularistic, differentially applied rule which creates advantages for squares and disadvantages for triangles in exchanges	Logical possibility that never occurred
2	Particularistic, differentially applied rule which limits exchanges to the lower class or among the upper class	Logical possibility that never occurred
1	Particularistic differentially applied rule which affects mobility	Logical possibility that never occurred
0	Upper class ends game (states or implies that lower class won the game)	Logical possibility that never occurred

Figure 5-1: Repression Index

Remember, in industrial societies class position after the second round of the game depended more upon trades than upon chip colors. In agrarian societies, possession of a yellow chip remained the central criterion for upper class membership, so raising the value of these chips constituted an overt benefit to upper class members. All rule changes in each society were coded on their degree of repression. The coded values of the *most* repressive rule changes and the *average* repressiveness of all rule changes were made part of the data set. These two measures were correlated .99 (.000).

Verbal Interactions

In order to keep track of verbal interactions between the two groups, a modified Bales (1950) Interaction Process Analysis coding scheme was used. The twelve categories of the Bales scheme were collapsed into four categories: positive emotions, declarative statements, questions, and negative emotions. During the rule change portion of the game, each verbal act that was initiated by one or more group members--and which appeared to be directed at the other group--was coded into one of the four categories. When possible, the actual statement was recorded in longhand in hopes of further exploring the social processes that were involved.

Collective Action

The variable of severity of collective action was conceptualized in terms of four dimensions derived from Russell (1974). These dimensions were: 1) Legality, 2) Aggressiveness, 3) Duration, and 4) Proportion of the group involved. Figure 5-2 outlines the coding criteria that were used to scale numerically each dimension. The index of *Collective Action* was computed by adding up the numerical values of each of the dimensions.

Dimension	Code	Description	Examples
Legality	4	Action is clearly outside of the current game rules	Showing chips (if Rule 1 is in effect). Triangles trading with Triangles (if rules forbid it)
	3	Action which is not prevented by the rules, but which is outside of the "umbrella rules" of the game; i.e., unwritten understandings necessary for play	Refusal to play. Leaving the classroom. Lying about scores. Triangles writing on chalkboard. Moving chairs closer together.
	2	Action which is quasi-legal. Further rule clarification would be necessary in order to determine legality/illegality	Triangles declaring themselves to be expelled from the game under Rule 7. Linking arms/hands.
	1	Action is clearly legal, but it uses a loophole in the rules.	Refusal to trade (legal by Rule 6) means that Triangles don't have to show their chips to Squares (New Rule 1).
			Triangles "tie-up" squares by holding their hands (Rule 2). Triangles never completing even one of four required trades with Squares (New Rule 6).
	0	Action is entirely within the rules.	Keeping Chips hidden (Rule 1). One for one trades (Rule 4).

Dimension	Code	Description
Duration = ending time of collective action minus beginning time		
Beginning time	4	Before the third round begins
	3	At the time the third round begins
	2	During the third round
	1	At the end of the third round
	0	Not at all

Ending time	5	Before the third round begins
	4	At the time the third round begins
	3	During the third round
	2	At the end of the third round
	1	After the end of the third round
	0	Not at all

Dimension	Code	Description
Proportion of lower class players involved	4	All
	3	Majority
	2	Many
	1	Few
	0	None

Dimension	Code	Description	Examples
Aggressiveness	4	Triangles are the aggressors in the squares' area	Triangles surround squares
	3	Triangles defend their own area	Triangles move chairs closer together. Triangles interlink arms.
	2	Triangles refuse to interact with squares	Triangles fold their arms when approached by squares.
	1	Triangles interact exclusively among themselves	Triangles ignore squares.
	0	Open trading takes place	Triangles acknowledge squares' presence. Triangles bargain with squares.

Inter-coder reliability for the coding of the four collective action categories exceeded .78 using Robinson's A.

Figure 5-2: Collective Action Codes

ROUND 3

As in earlier rounds, characteristics of the social structure, such as social class and group size, were used to predict status characteristics. A new variable of repressiveness replaced type of society (agrarian vs. industrial) because the rules were changed by the squares. Also, as in earlier rounds of STARPOWER, the block of variables called status characteristics was part of the analysis. Within this block, increases in scores by a group (mobility) were used to predict the number of players who would have changed groups, i.e., been motile. No players *actually* changed places after the third round of play, since the game was over. Scores were recorded on the chalkboard, as before. The number of motile players was estimated from the scores.

As in the earlier rounds, the block of variables of intergroup association was used in the analysis. These variables were measured as they were before. Immediately after the game ended, players completed a series of questionnaire items that tapped their perceptions of play during Round 3. As in previous rounds, the effects of social structure were assumed to be repeated upon these perceptions.

Postgame Perceptions

A number of items which appeared after earlier rounds of the game were repeated after the third round. The variables of perception of openness, rules in best interest of our group, desire for motility, ingroup privilege, outgroup deprivation, efficacy, and mistrust were operationalized in the same way as in the previous rounds.

The class organization variables of *plan of action* and *consensus on leadership* were measured in the same way as they were measured after Round 2. In addition to these two variables, a dummy variable of *continuity of leadership* was created. It was coded "0" if a *different* player was cited most often as the leader of the group for Round 2 versus Round 3. The variable was coded "1" if the same player was cited most frequently as the leader in both rounds.

The process of interaction between the two groups was measured with an item which asked players how the other group tried to influence them. This variable was measured by the item,

What is the best description of how the other group tried to influence us?"

The response scale contained three possible answers to the item,

_____ They tried to influence us without offering us any advantages or threatening any disadvantages.

_____ They tried to influence us by offering us advantages.

_____ They tried to influence us by threatening us with disadvantages.

The response scale was made into a dummy variable which was scored "0" for entries in either of the first two categories and "1" for an entry in the third category. This variable, *threats of disadvantages,* is predicted to affect the degree of perceived intergroup struggle.

A new item which appeared in the questionnaire after Round 3 measured the perceptions of perceived conflict between the two groups. This variable of intergroup struggle was measured by an item which asked,

> "What is the best description of relations between the two groups during this last round?"

The seven category response scale was anchored in the following way:

Peaceful   ___ ___ ___ ___ ___ ___ ___   Militant
Discussion   Struggle

Another new item was the degree of square responsiveness to suggestions from the lower class triangles. In order to measure the variable of *elite responsiveness*, players were asked,

> "How many of the triangles' proposals were incorporated into the rules by the squares?

All   ___ ___ ___ ___ ___ ___ ___   None

Scores of individuals were aggregated for each group.

Summary of Post Game Perceptions
Many studies of collective action have ended with the collective action itself. In this book the analysis represents an attempt to examine the effects of collective action upon subsequent perceptions of the players. Perceptions of intergroup struggle have their roots in the process of simulated conflict, and these perceptions are predicted to affect perceptions of square responsiveness and mistrust. Were the simulated society to continue, these variables would be the most important starting points for analysis of the next round of play.

CHAPTER SIX

HYPOTHESES TO BE TESTED IN THE STARPOWER SIMULATION

The hypotheses that are presented in this chapter have been derived from theory that was presented in Chapter Three. They are intended to make sense for class systems in the real world as well as for those in STARPOWER.

COMPONENTS OF THE THEORETICAL MODEL
Variables of the Social Structural Block

The first block of the Blau Model includes the three variables of the type of society (agrarian or industrial), the position of the social class (lower or upper), and the size of the social class (five to eighteen members). Game groups were randomly assigned to either the agrarian or the industrial version of STARPOWER. Within game groups, players were randomly assigned to either the upper or the lower class.

The type of society, a variable from the social structure block, is predicted to have an effect on status characteristics of the social classes in STARPOWER (see Figure 6-1). The status characteristics block is composed of the variables of mobility (changes in wealth), inequality in wealth, and motility (changes in social class membership).

Hypothesis 1-1a: Social classes in industrial societies will be distinguished by greater status characteristics (mobility, inequality, and motility) than will agrarian societies.

Hypothesis 1-1b: The greater the mobility of a social class, the greater will be the inequality within it.

Hypothesis 1-1c: The greater the inequality within a social class, the greater will be the number of players within it who will experience motility.

Intergroup Association

Three measures of trading in STARPOWER make up the index of intergroup association. These variables are the per capita number of intergroup associates, the per capita number of intergroup associations, and the ratio of

80

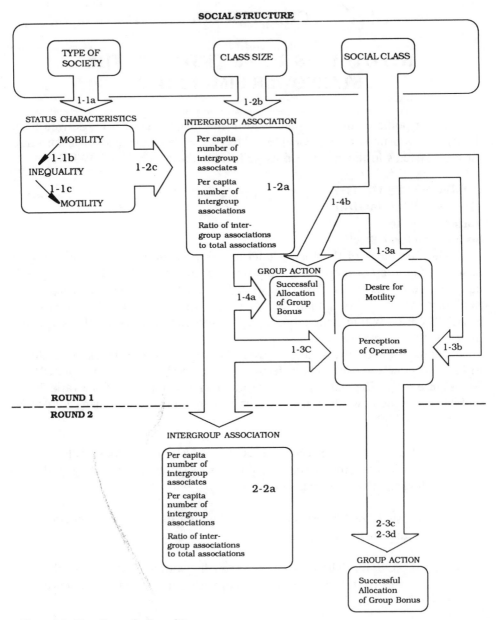

Figure 6-1: Hypotheses for Round 1

intergroup associations to total associations. The amount of intergroup association is predicted to vary with the size of the social class. Also, intergroup association is a mechanism by which status characteristics are linked to perceptions. As part of this process, status characteristics are predicted to influence intergroup association.

Hypothesis 1-2a: Per capita number of intergroup associates, per capita number of intergroup associations, and ratio of intergroup associations to total associations are predicted to be interrelated.

Hypothesis 1-2b: The greater the size of the social class, the greater will be the per capita intergroup association.

Hypothesis 1-2c: The greater the status characteristics, the greater will be the intergroup association.

Perceptions

Throughout the discussion on theory, perceptions and attitudes were conceptualized as resulting from interaction of individuals and groups within a social structure.

Desire for Motility

The desire for motility on the part of a player should be dependent upon which social class she chooses as a reference group. Until the lower class develops its own group organization, its members are more likely to identify upward, and upper class members are likely to identify with their own group. Since the questions were asked of players at the end of the first round of play, everyone knew that the object of the game was to get as many points as possible, and squares had the most points; therefore, the "winners" were going to come from the square group. Since this information emphasized the importance of being a square, social class should be a strong predictor of desire for motility in Round 1.

Perception of Openness

The perception of openness of a social system by participants should be influenced mostly by interaction patterns within the social system and by status characteristics. It also is possible that upper class members--afraid of the loss of their higher status--may perceive the social structure to be more open than do lower class members. Class position also is predicted to influence players' perceptions of openness of the class structure.

Hypothesis 1-3a: Lower class members will have a greater desire for motility than will upper class members.

Hypothesis 1-3b: Upper class members will have a greater perception of openness of the class structure than will lower class members.

Hypothesis 1-3c: The greater the intergroup association by a class, the greater the perception of openness of the class system by that class.

Group Organization
And Group Action

The first indication of emerging group organization in the game is the successful allocation of the three group bonus chips to group members. The theory predicts that perceptions by players in a social class will be the most important predictors of successful group action. In Round 1, the group bonus chips are allocated *before* perceptions of players are measured, so the prediction of group action from perceptions must wait until the second round. In lieu of perceptions as predictors of successful group action, intergroup association and social class will be used. Greater intergroup association is apt to lead to greater perception of openness, so individuals will focus on individual strategies. This orientation will make consensus more difficult to achieve in groups characterized by greater intergroup association. Also, lower classes in the game must decide whether to try to keep members in their group or to try to give them motility via the group bonus chips. This dilemma will make them less likely to allocate successfully the group bonus chips. On the other hand, it is clearer to members of upper classes that they should try to keep their members, so they do not face this dilemma. Members of upper classes are more likely to allocate successfully the group bonus chips.

> Hypothesis 1-4a: The greater the degree of intergroup association, the less likely is a social class to be successful in the allocation of the bonus chips.

> Hypothesis 1-4b: Upper classes are more likely to be successful in the group action of allocating the bonus chips than are lower classes.

ROUND 2
Social Structure

Social structure in Round 2 is conceptualized in the same way as it was in the previous round. Since the variables of social class, type of society, and class size have not changed, they are predicted to exert their influence as they did in Round 1 (see Figure 6-2).

Status Characteristics

The hypotheses are the same ones as those that were presented for the first round of the game.

> Hypothesis 2-1a: Social classes in industrial societies will be distinguished by greater status characteristics (mobility, inequality, and motility) than will agrarian societies.

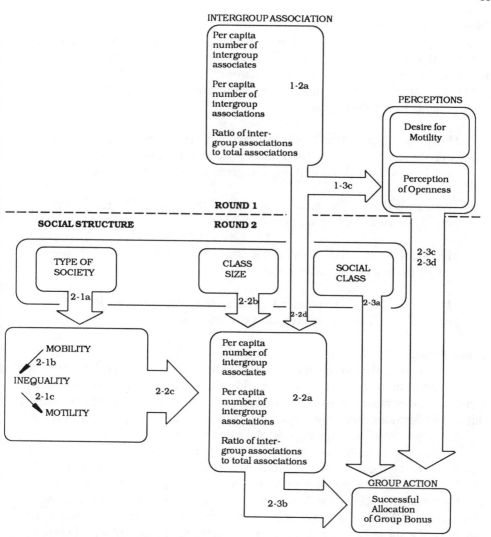

Figure 6-2: **Hypotheses for Round 2**

Hypothesis 2-1b: The greater the mobility of a social class, the greater will be the inequality within it.

Hypothesis 2-1c: The greater the inequality within a social class, the greater will be the number of players within it who will experience motility.

Intergroup Association

The predictions of intergroup association are the same as those for the first round--with one addition. It is probable that intergroup association from Round 1 will set a precedent for intergroup association in Round 2, and therefore, patterns of intergroup association in the second round will be predictable directly from patterns in the first round.

Hypothesis 2-2a: Per capita number of intergroup associates, per capita number of intergroup associations, and ratio of intergroup associations to total associations are predicted to be interrelated.

Hypothesis 2-2b: The greater the size of the group, the greater will be the per capita intergroup association.

Hypothesis 2-2c: The greater the status characteristics, the greater will be the intergroup association.

Hypothesis 2-2d: The greater the intergroup association in Round 1, the greater will be the intergroup association in Round 2.

Group Action

In Round 2, the groups have another opportunity to take collective action via the allocation of group bonus chips. In order to distribute them successfully, group members must come to a unanimous decision on the allocation of these chips. Furthermore, they must make this decision within the required time limit, and recipients must have the chips in their possession.

Desire for motility and perception of openness are predictors of group action. Both of these predictors were measured at the end of Round 1. The more that players in a group identify the system as an open one, and the more that they desire mobility, the less successful will be the group in allocating the bonus chips. Why? First, systems of stratification that are seen as open by members of a social class are likely to be characterized by individual achievement. This orientation inhibits the tendency of groups to share the chips among the most needy members, since it is more credible to attach blame to the individual for failure to achieve a high score than it is to blame the social system (Sennett and Cobb, 1972). Second, the more a group is characterized by a desire for mobility, the more the individuals within it may compete with each other for the chips, a process that interferes with group decision making.

Hypothesis 2-3a: Upper classes are more likely to be successful in the allocation of the group bonus chips than are lower classes.

Hypothesis 2-3b: The greater the intergroup association of a social class, the less likely is it to be successful in the allocation of the group bonus chips.

Hypothesis 2-3c: The greater the desire for motility by a lower class, the less likely it will be for that class to be successful in the allocation of the group bonus chips.

Hypothesis 2-3d: The greater the perception of openness by a social class, the less likely it will be for that class to be successful in the allocation of the group bonus chips.

THE END OF ROUND 2

The sequence of activities for players in the second round of the game is as follows: 1) trading period, 2) computation and reportage of scores, 3) group bonus and the addition of group bonus points to scores, and 4) motility, i.e., changes in group membership. During the instructions to players for the group bonus portion of Round 2, the idea was made clear to them that upper class members were going to make the rules for the third round of the game. Immediately after motility, players were asked to complete a number of questionnaire items on play of the game.

Perceptions

At this point in the game, social structural variables should have greater power to predict perceptions than they did in Round 1. In particular the variable of social class should have become more important to players, because the upper class players were going to make the rules!

Two new measures of player perceptions were used in the analysis for Round 2. They are perceptions of deprivation and perceptions of game rules being in the best interests of one's own group (see Figure 6-3).

Hypothesis 2-4a: The greater the perception of ingroup privilege the greater will be the perception of outgroup deprivation.

Hypothesis 2-4b: Upper classes will be characterized by less perceived deprivation than will lower classes.

Hypothesis 2-4c: Upper classes will be characterized by perceptions that game rules are more in the interest of their group than will lower classes.

Hypothesis 2-4d: Upper classes will be characterized by less desire for motility than will lower classes.

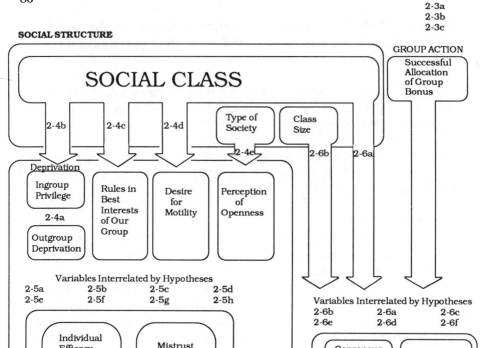

Figure 6-3: Hypotheses for Round 2 (continued)

Hypothesis 2-4e: Members of industrial societies will be characterized by perceptions of greater openness of the class system than will members of agrarian societies.

Hypothesis 2-4e is slightly different than the one for the last round. By the end of Round 2, players should see clearly that they *can* get ahead in the industrial version and that they cannot get ahead in the agrarian version.

Attitudes

Two attitudinal measures are new to the model after Round 2 of the game. Individual efficacy and mistrust have roots in values and beliefs, so they should be related to the perception variables. As individuals in a group are less desirous of motility, they should be oriented more to their own social class as a group. Desire for motility puts players in a situation of individual competition with other players. This competition is especially keen with members of the other class, so they may tend to mistrust them more than do players who do not desire motility.

Perceptions of greater openness will be found in industrial societies (see Hypothesis 2-4e above). Perceptions of greater openness may be reflective of an achievement orientation in which those who work the hardest legitimately earn the most points; therefore, perceptions of greater openness are predicted to result in greater efficacy and less mistrust of the other group. In fact, perceptions that things are going well for a class are predicted to increase individual efficacy and decrease mistrust across the board.

Hypothesis 2-5a: The more a social class is characterized by perceptions of deprivation on the part of its members, the less it will be characterized by an attitude of efficacy.

Hypothesis 2-5b: The more a social class is characterized by the belief of its members that the game rules are in the best interests of the class, the more it will be characterized by an attitude of efficacy.

Hypothesis 2-5c: The more a social class is characterized by a desire for motility on the part of its members, the more it will be characterized by an attitude of efficacy.

Hypothesis 2-5d: The more a social class is characterized by a perception of openness of the class system on the part of its members, the more it will be characterized by an attitude of efficacy.

Hypothesis 2-5e: The more a social class is characterized by perceptions of deprivation on the part of its members, the more it will be characterized by an attitude of mistrust of the other social class.

Hypothesis 2-5f: The more a social class is characterized by the belief of its members that the game rules are in the best interests of the class, the more it will be characterized by an attitude of mistrust of the other social class.

Hypothesis 2-5g: The more a social class is characterized by a desire for motility on the part of its members, the more it will be characterized by an attitude of mistrust of the other social class.

Hypothesis 2-5h: The more a social class is characterized by a perception of openness of the class system on the part of its members, the less it will be characterized by an attitude of mistrust of the other social class.

Perceptions of Group Organization

The questionnaire contained two measures of perceived class organization--consensus on leadership in the group and perceived plan of action by the group. Upper classes had an easier task in maintaining class boundaries than did lower classes because they didn't have to face the dilemma of whether to orient the class to upward mobility or toward the retention of class members. Also, larger groups are proportionally more difficult to organize than are smaller ones. Finally, classes which have undertaken successful action in Round 1 already have overcome at least some problems of consensus, and they have acted in a coordinated manner, so they are more likely to be perceived by their members as having developed leadership and a plan of action.

> Hypothesis 2-6a: Upper classes will be characterized by their members as having greater consensus on leadership than will lower classes.

> Hypothesis 2-6b: The larger the size of a social class, the greater will be the consensus on leadership by its members.

> Hypothesis 2-6c: Successful allocation of the group bonus by a class in the first round of the game will lead members of the class to characterize it as having greater consensus on leadership than classes that did not successfully allocate the group bonus.

> Hypothesis 2-6d: Upper classes are more likely to be characterized by their members as having a plan of action than are lower classes.

> Hypothesis 2-6e: The larger the size of a social class, the more likely are members to characterize it as having a plan of action.

> Hypothesis 2-6f: Successful allocation of the group bonus by a class in the first round of the game will lead members of the class to characterize it as having a plan of action.

THE RULE CHANGE
PORTION OF THE GAME

After the second round of STARPOWER, members of both social classes are reminded that the upper class players have the authority to change the game rules for the third round. Both classes are told that the lower class triangles may suggest possible rule changes, but the upper class squares actually have the authority to implement the changes.

The main dependent variables in this part of the analysis are the number of rule changes made by upper class members and the repressiveness of the new rules. Predictor variables include characteristics of social structure, perceptions of play, and interactions between the two social classes. Since squares have the exclusive right to make rules, the variable of social class will not be a part of the analysis.

For the first time in the game, the two classes which make up each society have functional differences in the form of complete rule making authority of the upper class versus no authority of the lower class. The units of analysis now are the sixty-four societies, not the 128 social classes that make them up.

Number of Rule Changes

It is predicted that square groups will implement more rules in the agrarian than in the industrial version. Why? The rules in the agrarian version already are repressive. Relaxation of these rules would point up the unfairness of the system, so squares are likely to make a *greater* number of repressive rules. Also, the larger the square group, the more difficult it will be to coordinate the rule change procedures, so the less likely it will be for them to make rules (see Figure 6-4). Note: Since this portion of the game is after Round 2 and before Round 3, the hypotheses are referred to as "2/3."

Hypothesis 2/3-1a: Upper class members in the agrarian version of the game are likely to make more changes in the rules than are upper class members in the industrial version.

Hypothesis 2/3-1b: The larger the upper class, the fewer rule changes it will make.

Hypothesis 2/3-1c: The more that an upper class is characterized by an attitude of efficacy on the part of its members, the greater the number of rule changes it will make.

Hypothesis 2/3-1d: The more that an upper class is characterized by an attitude of mistrust of the other group, the greater the number of rule changes it will make.

Hypothesis 2/3-1e: The more that an upper class is characterized by a consensus on leadership, the fewer rule changes it will make.

Hypothesis 2/3-1f: The more that an upper class is characterized by a plan of action, the fewer rule changes it will make.

Repressiveness

Due to the fact that agrarian societies are more likely to rely on the rules to control members of the lower class, members of the upper class in agrarian societies are more likely to make rules which are more repressive than are members of the upper class in industrial societies. Also, upper class members of larger social classes are predicted to make rules that are less repressive than

90

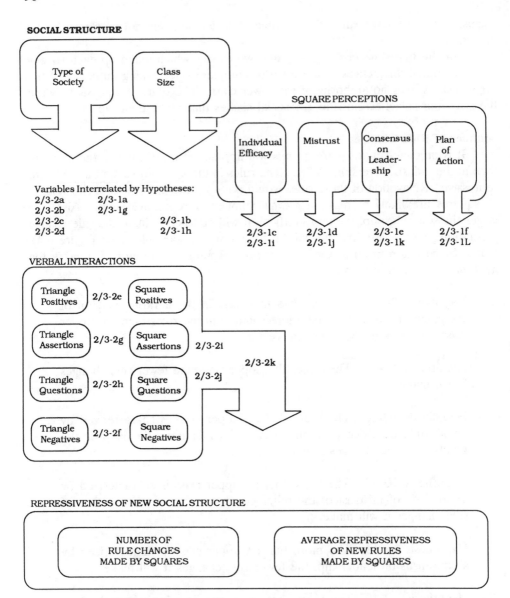

SOCIAL STRUCTURE

Type of Society

Class Size

SQUARE PERCEPTIONS

Individual Efficacy

Mistrust

Consensus on Leadership

Plan of Action

Variables Interrelated by Hypotheses:
2/3-2a   2/3-1a
2/3-2b   2/3-1g
2/3-2c   2/3-1b
2/3-2d   2/3-1h

2/3-1c   2/3-1d   2/3-1e   2/3-1f
2/3-1i   2/3-1j   2/3-1k   2/3-1L

VERBAL INTERACTIONS

Triangle Positives   2/3-2e   Square Positives

Triangle Assertions   2/3-2g   Square Assertions   2/3-2i

Triangle Questions   2/3-2h   Square Questions   2/3-2j

2/3-2k

Triangle Negatives   2/3-2f   Square Negatives

REPRESSIVENESS OF NEW SOCIAL STRUCTURE

NUMBER OF RULE CHANGES MADE BY SQUARES

AVERAGE REPRESSIVENESS OF NEW RULES MADE BY SQUARES

Figure 6-4: Hypotheses for Rule Changes

upper class members of smaller social classes. Finally, the number of rule changes is predicted to be related to the average repressiveness of the rule changes.

Hypothesis 2/3-1g: Upper class members of agrarian societies are predicted to make rules that are more repressive than are upper class members of industrial societies.

Hypothesis 2/3-1h: The larger the upper class, the less repressive will be the rule changes it will make.

The combination of number of rule changes and repressiveness of the changes may be referred to as the repressiveness of the new social structure of STARPOWER that was created by the upper class squares. Efficacy and mistrust are predicted to affect repressiveness. Also, to the extent that upper classes are organized, they are likely to change the social structure to make it more repressive.

Hypothesis 2/3-1i: The greater the attitude of efficacy on the part of members of the upper class, the more repressive will be the new social structure that they create.

Hypothesis 2/3-1j: The greater the attitude of mistrust on the part of members of the upper class, the more repressive will be the new social structure that they create.

Hypothesis 2/3-1k: The greater the consensus on leadership in the upper class, the more repressive will be the new social structure that they create.

Hypothesis 2/3-1l: The more that upper class members perceive that they have a plan of action, the more repressive will be the new social structure that they create.

Verbal Interactions

During the rule change portion of the game, each time someone in one social class said something that appeared to be directed at the other group, the act was coded into one of the four Bales IPA categories.

Since the rules of the agrarian version of the game kept lower class triangles from attaining upward mobility, these tensions should have been verbalized by them during the rule change portion of the game. Triangles are predicted to suggest new rules in the form of both declarative acts and questions. Furthermore, tensions over the restrictive social structure are predicted to be expressed as acts with negative emotion by both groups.

Hypothesis 2/3-2a: During the rule making, a greater number of emotion positive statements will be made by members of the lower class in industrial societies than in agrarian societies.

Hypothesis 2/3-2b: During the rule making, a greater number of declarative statements will be made by members of the lower class in agrarian societies than in industrial societies.

Hypothesis 2/3-2c: During the rule making, a greater number of questions will be asked of squares by members of the lower class in agrarian societies than in industrial societies.

Hypothesis 2/3-2d: During the rule making, a greater number of negative statements will be made by members of the lower class in agrarian societies than in industrial societies.

Social classes are apt to reciprocate in their verbal interactions. For instance, it seems reasonable to predict that the number of emotion negative verbal acts by the lower class will be matched by the number of emotion negative acts by the upper class, a negative interaction cycle. Also, when members of the lower class suggest new rules, upper class members are likely to respond with emotion negative acts, so the number of lower class questions should be correlated with the number of upper class emotion negative acts. Lower class questions are apt to evoke upper class answers, so numbers of acts in these two categories are predicted to be correlated. Upper class statements about new rules are predicted to trigger lower class emotion negative acts. Finally, upper class questions are likely to be seen as attempts at responsiveness by the upper class, so they are predicted to be met with lower class emotion positive acts.

Hypothesis 2/3-2e: The greater the number of lower class emotion positive verbal acts, the greater will be the number of upper class emotion positive acts.

Hypothesis 2/3-2f: The greater the number of lower class emotion negative verbal acts, the greater will be the number of upper class emotion negative verbal acts.

Hypothesis 2/3-2g: The greater the number of lower class declarative acts, the greater will be the number of upper class emotion negative verbal acts.

Hypothesis 2/3-2h: The greater the number of lower class questions, the greater will be the number of upper class declarative acts.

Hypothesis 2/3-2i: The greater the number of upper class statements, the greater the number of lower class emotion negative verbal acts.

Hypothesis 2/3-2j: The greater the number of upper class questions, the greater the number of lower class emotion positive verbal acts.

Hypothesis 2/3-2k: The greater the volume of interaction in a society, the less the repressiveness.

Collective Action

Severity of collective action was measured by using the four dimensions of legality, aggressiveness, duration, and proportion of the group involved (Russell, 1974). A number of factors are predicted to influence collective action (see Figure 6-5). First, agrarian societies are more likely to experience collective action than are industrial societies. Since larger groups are more difficult to organize, the larger the group, the less severe should be the collective action. As upper class groups create new social structures which are more repressive, the more severe should be the collective action by lower class members. As lower class members are more efficacious and mistrustful of upper class members, the more severe should be the collective action. Even if communication between the two groups is rancorous, the more of it that takes place, the less severe should be the collective action. The more the lower class is characterized by consensus on leadership and a plan of action, the more severe should be the collective action.

Hypothesis 2/3-3a: Agrarian societies are likely to undergo more severe collective action than are industrial societies.

Hypothesis 2/3-3b: The greater the size of the social classes, the less severe will be the collective action.

Hypothesis 2/3-3c: The greater the repressiveness of the new social structure, the more severe will be the collective action.

Hypothesis 2/3-3d: The greater the efficacy of the lower class, the more severe will be the collective action.

Hypothesis 2/3-3e: The greater the mistrust of the upper class by the lower class, the more severe will be the collective action.

Hypothesis 2/3-3f: The greater the volume of interaction between the two classes, the less severe will be the collective action.

Hypothesis 2/3-g: The greater the consensus on leadership by the lower class, the more severe will be the collective action.

Hypothesis 2/3-h: The greater the plan of action by the lower class, the more severe will be the collective action.

ROUND 3
Status Characteristics

As in earlier rounds, characteristics of the social structure will be used to predict status characteristics. The variables of social class, societal openness (a measure that replaces society type; the inverse of repressiveness), and class size

94

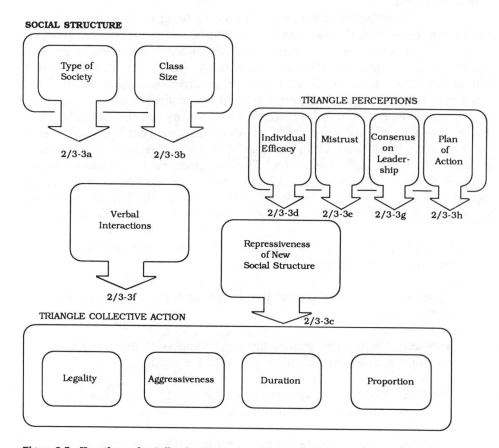

Figure 6-5: Hypotheses for Collective Action

are used to predict status characteristics of mobility, inequality, and motility. Note that the units of analysis are the social classes once again (see Figure 6-6).

Hypothesis 3-1a: The greater the openness of a society, the greater will be status characteristics (mobility, inequality, and motility) within classes of that society.

Hypothesis 3-1b: The greater the mobility of a social class, the greater will be the inequality within it.

Hypothesis 3-1c: The greater the inequality within a social class, the greater will be the number of players within it who will experience motility.

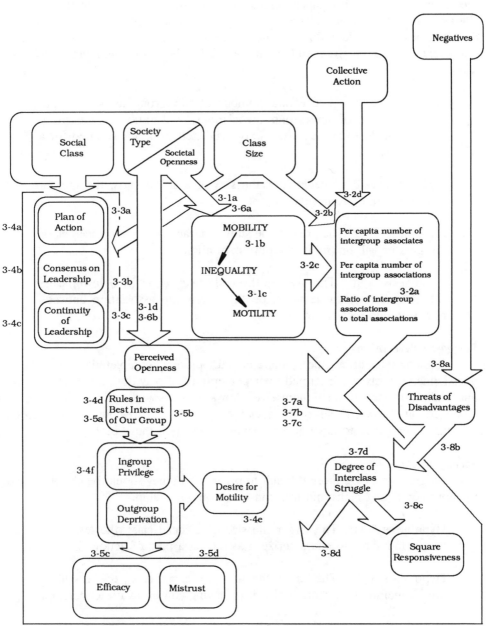

Figure 6-6: Hypotheses For Round 3

Intergroup Association

The size of a society should be a predictor of intergroup association, and the components of this block should be interrelated. Furthermore, status characteristics should be related to intergroup association as before. Finally, collective action should influence intergroup association. Rancorous conflict is not likely to result in free and open association between members of *warring* classes.

> Hypothesis 3-2a: Per capita number of intergroup associates, per capita number of intergroup associations, and ratio of intergroup associations to total associations are predicted to be interrelated for a social class.

> Hypothesis 3-2b: The greater the size of a social class, the greater will be the intergroup association.

> Hypothesis 3-2c: The greater the status characteristics of a social class, the greater will be the intergroup association.

> Hypothesis 3-2d: The greater the collective action by a lower class within a society, the less will be the intergroup association between classes within that society.

Postgame Perceptions

Immediately after the game ended, players completed a series of questionnaire items which tapped their perceptions of play during the third round and their attitudes toward themselves, toward the social class to which they belonged, and toward the other social class. As in previous rounds, social structure is expected to have an important effect upon these perceptions.

Social Structure

Larger classes are more difficult to organize, so they should be characterized by more conflicting plans and less consensus on leadership.

> Hypothesis 3-3a: The larger the size of a social class, the less likely are its members to characterize it as having a plan of action.

> Hypothesis 3-3b: The larger the size of a social class, the less likely are its members to characterize it as having consensus on leadership.

> Hypothesis 3-3c: The larger the size of a social class, the less likely is it to have continuity of leadership.

Social class is predicted to have an effect upon a variable of continuity of leadership, a dummy variable which is scored "1" when the player who gets the most leadership votes in Round 2 also is the person who receives the most votes at the end of play. In the earlier rounds of the game, leadership takes the form of helping to coordinate the group to follow effectively the instructions of the game administrator in order to allocate the group bonus successfully. Later in the game, changing the framework of the rules for the upper class is closer to earlier tasks than is organizing the lower class in reaction to the new rules, i. e., creatively planning alternative courses of action. The upper classes can handle new tasks more easily within an existing organizational framework, while lower classes need to change their group organization (at least in terms of leadership) in order to meet the new contingencies created by the rule changes.

As in the earlier rounds of the game, perceptions that the game rules favor the upper class can lead players to feel that lower class members are deprived and that upper class members are privileged.

Social class also is predicted to be related to perceptions of the rules being in the best interest of the group, since after the rule change portion of the game, the rules are even more likely to favor the upper class squares than prior to the rule changes. Social class also is predicted to be related to the desire for mobility. Finally, social class is predicted to be related to perceptions of deprivation.

Hypothesis 3-4a: Upper classes are more likely to be characterized by their members as having a plan of action than are lower classes.

Hypothesis 3-4b: Upper classes will be characterized by their members as having greater consensus on leadership than will lower classes.

Hypothesis 3-4c: Upper classes are more likely to have continuity of leadership than are lower classes.

Hypothesis 3-4d: Upper classes will be characterized by perceptions that game rules are more in the interest of their group than will lower classes.

Hypothesis 3-4e: Upper classes will be characterized by less desire for motility than will lower classes.

Hypothesis 3-4f: Upper classes will be characterized by less perceived deprivation than will lower classes.

Hypothesis 3-5a: The greater the perception by a class that the game rules are in its best interests, the more it will be characterized by perceptions of privilege. Conversely, the greater the perception by a class that the game rules are in the best interests of the other class, the more it will be characterized by perceptions of deprivation.

Hypothesis 3-5b: The greater the perception by a class that the game rules are in its best interests, the less it will be characterized by desire for motility.

Perceptions of privilege and deprivation are predicted to be related to attitudes of efficacy and mistrust.

Hypothesis 3-5c: The greater the feelings of ingroup privilege by a social class, the more the class will be characterized by the attitude of efficacy.

Hypothesis 3-5d: The greater the feelings of ingroup privilege by a social class, the more the class will be characterized by the attitude of mistrust of the other class.

Even after the rule changes, the effect of the agrarian and industrial types of society still will be felt by social classes in the game. It is predicted that industrial societies will be perceived as more open than will agrarian societies.

Hypothesis 3-6: Societies that began as industrial ones will be perceived by their members as more open than those that began as agrarian societies.

The predictions of relations between intergroup association and other variables in the model remain basically the same as in other rounds of the game. The exception to this similarity is the addition of a new variable of perception of intergroup struggle that was added to the analysis. As intergroup association increases, the perception of intergroup struggle decreases.

Hypothesis 3-7a: The greater the intergroup association of a social class, the less the class will be characterized by perceptions of deprivation.

Hypothesis 3-7b: The greater the intergroup association of a social class, the more the class will be characterized by perceptions that the game rules are in its best interests.

Hypothesis 3-7c: The greater the intergroup association of a social class, the more the class will be characterized by the desire for motility.

Hypothesis 3-7d: The greater the intergroup association of a social class, the less the class will be characterized by perceptions of interclass struggle.

Interaction

Patterns of interaction are predicted to influence perceptions of the relations between two social classes.

Hypothesis 3-8a: The greater the number of negative interactions between the two social classes, the more the social classes will be characterized by perceptions that the other class tried to influence them through threats of disadvantages.

Hypothesis 3-8b: The more that the society is characterized by perceptions that members of an outgroup tried to influence members of an ingroup by "threats of disadvantages," the more the society will be characterized by perceptions of interclass struggle.

Perceptions of intergroup struggle can lead to perceptions that upper class members are not responsive to the wishes of members of the lower classes in the game. Perceptions of intergroup struggle also can lead to an attitude of mistrust of the other group.

Hypothesis 3-8c: The greater the perception of interclass struggle, the less will be the perceptions of upper class responsiveness.

Hypothesis 3-8d: The greater is the perception of intergroup struggle by a social class, the more likely it is to be characterized by the attitude of mistrust of the other class.

SUMMARY OF THE
HYPOTHESES

The starting point for the research was the creation of the agrarian and the industrial versions of STARPOWER. The hypotheses attempted to predict how the stratification system of each type of society worked, and how collective action was related to societal type.

Round 1

In Round 1, the type of society predicted status characteristics, a block of variables that included mobility, inequality, and motility. Status characteristics and group size predicted the amount of intergroup association, a block of three variables. Finally, social class predicted player desire for motility and perception of openness of the social system. Intergroup association also predicted the perception of openness.

Round 2

In the second round of the game, social class and type of society were predicted to affect status characteristics. The type of society was predicted to have an effect upon intergroup association, as was intergroup association from the first round. Perceptions from the end of Round 1 were predicted to affect successful group action in the second round of the game. At the end of Round 2, information was gathered on perceptions of players. A considerable number of predictions were made concerning the effects of social class, type of society, and group size on perceptions of the game and attitudes toward the other social class.

Rule Change Portion
Of the Game

In the rule change portion of the game attention focused on the prediction of repressiveness. Type of society, size of the social class, upper class efficacy, mistrust, leadership, and interaction between the two groups were used to predict repressiveness. A second major group of predictions focused on collective action. Type of society, size of the social class, lower class efficacy and mistrust, leadership, interaction patterns, and repressiveness were used to predict collective action.

Round 3

Collective action was predicted to affect intergroup association in Round 3. Type of society was predicted to affect status characteristics and intergroup association. Social class was predicted to affect status characteristics and perceptions. Size of the social class was predicted to affect class organization and leadership. Intergroup association and interaction between the two classes were predicted to affect perceptions. Perceptions were predicted to affect attitudes of efficacy and mistrust.

CHAPTER SEVEN

RESEARCH PROCEDURES

The research methods that were used with STARPOWER were developed through much trial and error. At all times the procedures represented a conscious attempt to balance the roles of students *as learners* with those of students as *research participants*. This equilibrium is the key to research with gamed simulations, because if the learning emphasis is forsaken, the play spirit too will be lost, and the exercise will become sterile, preoccupied with verification. On the other hand, if the scientific emphasis of the exercise is abandoned, it will become idiosyncratic, unworthy of scholarly attention. The key to the maintenance of this balance is the effective grafting of the procedures to the simulation. Earlier in this text, gamed simulations were described as hybrids. A certain vigor or robustness of this hybrid is necessary in order for it to support a research design. Though no formal measures of robustness of a simulation have been developed, most gamers would agree that STARPOWER is among the most robust of gamed simulations.

THE CLASSROOM GROUPS

Forty-seven classes were used in this study. They were chosen on an availability basis from among undergraduate sociology and social anthropology courses at five colleges and universities. In instances where class size, room availability, and time considerations were favorable for breaking up a class into comparable groups, students were randomly assigned to agrarian or industrial versions of the game (as well as to the square or triangle groups within them). Thirteen classes were divided into two or more comparable parts to produce thirty game groups. Thirty-four additional classes were left intact. Each of them was randomly assigned to play either the agrarian or the industrial version of the game. The final data set was made up of sixty-four game groups each of which was comprised of ten to thirty-seven players. Within each game group, individual players were randomly assigned to either the square group (upper class) or to the triangle group (lower class). The original three social classes of STARPOWER were limited to two groups as an aid to observation. Although this modification of the game never has been put to a systematic test, most likely it operates in a manner that is similar to the three-class version.

PLAYER CHARACTERISTICS

Players were college and university undergraduates. Though data were not gathered on the demographics of players, they were mostly under thirty years of age, slightly more female than male, and predominantly white and middle class. A total of 1213 players made up the sixty-four game groups and 128 social classes of the data set.

101

SIZE OF SOCIETIES

Careful attention was paid to the sizes of the game groups within the agrarian and industrial versions of the game in order to insure that each game group of the agrarian version was matched by a comparably sized game group of the industrial version. Figure 7-1 shows the sizes of the game groups of the agrarian and industrial versions of STARPOWER. The reader can see that some variation in the absolute sizes of the large game groups occurred. The thirty-two groups which played under the agrarian rules averaged 18.78 players per group, and the thirty-two groups of the industrial version averaged 19.12 players per group. Robinson's A (see Robinson, 1957), a measure of exact agreement, was used to test further the correspondence between the groups in each experimental treatment. The $\underline{A}$ value of .92 indicates a very high level of agreement in group sizes.

SIZE OF SOCIAL CLASSES

Within each game group, players were randomly assigned to the upper or lower class. In groups which had an odd number of players, the "extra" player was assigned to the lower class. Game materials were put into white business envelopes prior to play. Envelopes that were to be given to players in the upper class were marked differently than those of lower class players. The game administrator(s) easily could tell them apart, but players could not. No player ever asked about this difference. Before play, more than enough envelopes were prepared for the expected number of students who would play the game. In the classroom, the administrator arranged the chairs into two circular groups of equal size.

At the time that the class was to begin, she counted the number of students who were in attendance and took the *extra* envelopes for both upper and lower class members from the box in which they were carried. Quickly she shuffled the remaining envelopes without taking them out of the box. The envelopes in their "new" random order were passed out to students. The administrator had no choice in which student received which envelope. As she moved around the two groups of chairs in the most efficient manner, the "next" student always received the "next" envelope.

After all envelopes were distributed, players were told which group of chairs belonged to the squares and which one belonged to the triangles. Players were instructed to pin on the triangular or square badges and to take seats in the appropriate set of chairs. Next, the remaining envelopes were returned to the box. They were placed in alternating order (square, triangle, square, etc.).

LATE ARRIVING PLAYERS

Class time was precious, so the administrator needed to start the game as soon as possible after the class began. Inevitably, a few students entered the classroom late. If they came in during the pregame briefing, they were given the "next" envelope from the box, and they were told where to sit. They listened to

Agrarian Version	Industrial Version
10	10
10	11
11	11
11	11
12	12
12	12
12	13
12	13
13	14
14	15
15	15
16	16
16	17
16	17
17	17
18	18
18	18
19	18
19	19
19	19
20	19
20	19
20	21
21	24
23	24
26	26
26	26
30	27
30	28
31	29
31	36
<u>33</u>	<u>37</u>

	Agrarian	Industrial
Number of Players	601	612
Number of Games	32	32
Mean Number of Players	18.78	19.12
Standard Deviation	6.71	6.92

Figure 7-1: Numbers of Players in the Agrarian and the Industrial Versions of STARPOWER

the remainder of the briefing with the other players. If they came in during the first five minutes of Round 1 the administrator gave them the "next" envelope, and then she recounted briefly the basic rules and object of the game. Their badge was pinned on, and they were encouraged to play slowly and to try to learn about the game from the other members of their group. If players came in later than the halfway point of the first round, they became informal observers. They were told to watch the game carefully. During the debriefing, these players were asked to report what they had seen.

The procedures generated square and triangle groups which were equal in size (or ones in which the lower class was larger by one player). Occasionally, in the confusion of beginning the game, the administrator made an incorrect count of students present, or she assigned the "odd" player to the upper class. Rarely did the administrator assign a new player to a lower class which already had the extra or "odd" player. As long as the group was not a small one, the one or two players which "lopsided" a group did not alter the percentages of players in each group to a large extent, so these plays were retained in the data set. Once a player saw the chips for one group, the administrator dared not jeopardize the entire play by giving him a different envelope containing chips for the other group. Only one game group had to be dropped from the data set due to problems in randomly assigning students to the upper or lower class.

STARPOWER AND THE SOCIOLOGY AND SOCIAL ANTHROPOLOGY CURRICULUM

With one exception, all courses which generated data for this research dealt with topics concerning stratification, so generally the game matched the curriculum at least to a moderate degree. Instructors and their classes were provided with a gaming experience in exchange for the data that was gathered from the exercise. Sometimes the timing of the play in the course did not coincide with the timing of the stratification topic. Everyone seemed to enjoy the game; however, if gamed simulations are to achieve their full potential as educational experiences and also as research tools, they must be sequenced carefully in the curriculum so that teaching and data gathering optimally complement each other.

GAME ADMINISTRATION

The first twenty-two plays set were conducted by one administrator and one observer. During group bonus rounds and the rule change portion of the game, the administrator observed one of the groups, and the observer took notes on the other group. Administrator and observer were randomly assigned to observe the square and triangle groups. Additional experience with data gathering revealed that the administration and observation of the game could be carried out by a single person who performed both functions. Fifteen of the plays in the current data set were administered and observed by persons other than the author. These helpers were trained as observers first, and then after they became familiar with the administration procedures they were given the responsibility of conducting the game and observing it.

Instructions to Players

From a research standpoint, two of the most crucial requirements of the administrator role are giving the instructions and observing the rule making collective action. In this research an emphasis was placed on naturalness of presentation on the part of the administrator, so that players would feel at ease with the game. The transcript containing the instructions appeared in Chapter Four. Administrators followed the script from memory. The decision not to read the script was made because it could inhibit spontaneity. Plummer (1976) took an entirely different tack with regard to presenting rules. He videotaped the entire administration of STARPOWER. This procedure insured absolute standardization of instructions, and it allowed absolute control of the time that was used in each portion of the game. Control of time was of critical importance to Plummer, since he was interested in its distortion by players (see Chapter Two).

IDENTIFICATION TAGS

In both the first and second editions of STARPOWER, Shirts used blank tags in the form of triangles, circles, and squares to identify group membership. When scores were tallied on the chalkboard for each group, initials of players' names were used to identify them. In pretesting for this research it was found that tallying the scores moved faster if the badge contained the player identification on it. Therefore, one or two letters of the alphabet were added to the triangular shaped tags, and one or two numbers were added to the square shaped tags. During the first trading round, the administrator entered the "game identities" of all players into their respective groups on the chalkboard. No time was wasted in this process, since players continued to trade while the numbers and letters on their tags were being written on the chalkboard. Entering scores beside these identities became a shorter, easier task than before. Also, it avoided the possible confusion due to two players having the same initials. Furthermore, these game identities were easy for players to code onto their own scoresheets in order to keep track of the number of players with whom they traded. The tags also allowed group members to identify group leaders on the questionnaires after Rounds 2 and 3. Finally, the identities helped observers to keep track of players who become involved in verbal interaction and collective action.

During the construction of the tags, all number "ones" and letter "I's" (and some other ambiguities) were removed in order to lessen confusion in reading the tags. Reading them was not a problem for anyone as long as the player was facing them. Unanticipated problems did occur in reading players' scoresheets. Players who did not write clearly and who became highly involved in trading sometimes wrote illegible letter "Z's", number "2's", letter "O's" and number "0's." Painstaking cross-checking of all other scoresheets for a play cleared up this confusion. Cross checking was made possible from the following facts: each time player "letter O" traded with player "number 2", the number "2" should have appeared as a trading partner on O's scoresheet, and the letter "O" should have appeared on number 2's scoresheet. If an entry couldn't be read on one scoresheet, it appeared on another.

PLAYER'S LOGS

The scoresheets which were created by the researcher for players of STARPOWER consisted of three sections for keeping score and two or three sections for players' responses to questionnaire items (see Appendix A). The sections for keeping score were used by players continually throughout each trading round. Players began by entering their tag numbers or letters on the scoresheets. Later, these codes became the keys to aggregating the information in the logs for triangle and square groups. Upon completion of a trade, the players entered the tag number or letter of any trading partner(s) into a box on the scoresheet. This entry allowed players to keep track of the number of trades they completed in order to compute the trading bonus. Entries in these boxes also allowed the researcher to compute the numbers and ratios of intragroup and intergroup trades ("associations" in Blau's, 1977, terms).

At the end of the first trading round, players filled in some of the other boxes on the scoresheet. They entered the values of their current set of chips, bonus for same colors, and bonus for number of trades. They added these values together and verbally reported the sum when the administrator called their tag numbers or letters.

After the group bonus portion of the game, each player completed the information in the group bonus box and figured his total score for the round. After each round of the game, players were asked to complete the questionnaire items in their Player's Log.

During the middle phase of the data gathering, questionnaire items from the end of Round 1 were omitted in order to save time and because the ability of players to understand the game at such an early juncture seemed to be limited. Later the items were reinstated because they became important in the theory that was being developed to explain play of the game. Because of this vacillation, several findings for Round 1 are based on a smaller number of cases than those for the rest of the research.

After motile players changed tags and seats, all players again entered their tag numbers or letters in the box on the scoresheet for Round 2. A *difference* in these entries from Round 1 to Round 2 indicated that a player was motile. The actual measurement of motility was straightforward in the first round. By the second round, coders had to resort to a more complex code in order to identify a triangle or a square because players may have changed groups, but the same set of identification tags still were being used in the game. By the third round of the game, players may have switched groups again. A total of eight codes was necessary to cover all possibilities--no motility, one motility, or two. These codes proved to be highly susceptible to error on the part of the coder. Due the central importance of motility to the study, these codes were checked three times. Useful crosschecks included the question on the group's leader, the other scoresheets, or (as mentioned above) if all else failed, the scores for all players were checked in order to reconstruct the complete motility picture. With over 1200 cases in the data set, completion of the final check required five working days!

Players carried forward their scores on the scoresheet from the first round to the second. This procedure represented "investment." They began a second trading round with the same chips in their envelopes. After Round 2, players completed a second set of questionnaire items. If a third round of the game occurred, the sequence of activities was the same as that in the first and second rounds.

TIMING OF ROUNDS

The original rules of STARPOWER suggested an approximate length of time for each portion of the game. The lengths of these portions were standardized as part of the research design, and a kitchen timer with an audible bell was used to time the rounds. Trading rounds were nine minutes long, and bonus rounds were three minutes in length. Players often consulted the timer in order to make strategic decisions during trading or to try to force consensus during the bonus rounds.

STANDARDIZED
BONUS ROUNDS

The original game rules did not specify how the bonus chips were to be delivered to the groups by the administrator. Pretesting showed that if a player was handed the chips (or if they were placed near him) inevitably he received at least one bonus chip. The problem was overcome by placing the chips on the floor as close to the center of the group as possible. Also, successful allocation of the bonus chips was clarified to mean that players must have the chips in their possession in order to receive credit for them. This procedure forced the groups to take action by distributing the chips to the recipients rather than merely by making the decision on which player(s) would receive them.

ROUND 3

The wording of the instructions for the original version of STARPOWER was not completely clear on an expected sequence of activities. Shirts told administrators to expect repressive rules and collective action. He advised, "Stop the game when it is evident that the squares have made rules which are so unfair that the groups can't or won't continue (Shirts, 1969: 6)." Pretesting showed that this guideline encouraged the administrator to stop the game too soon. Typically, before the third round, the squares are the all-powerful rulemakers. When they try to start the third round, they need compliance from the triangles. This change can provide an opportunity for triangles to engage in collective action which would be missed if the game was ended when triangles voiced their displeasure over the repressive rules. Also, actually playing under the new rules allows the assessment of their impact on play in terms of player action and subsequent motility.

RULE CHANGES

In the original version of STARPOWER, squares created the new rules, and then they announced them to the other players. In order to make this process easier to study, square players were told that changes must be made on the chalkboard, so everyone could see them. The eraser and chalk were placed in the center of the square group. The administrator/observer retired to the back of the room to take notes on rule changes, verbal interaction and collective action.

Before pretesting, it seemed as if the observer would be swamped by too much action, and indeed when the twelve-category Bales system was used in the pretesting, often he was overwhelmed. As soon as the current system evolved, data overload ceased to be a problem. After much revision during pretesting--and with the classroom as the guide--a method of combining the Bales IPA (1950/ 1970) with longhand notes was devised. Bales' twelve categories were reduced to four, and each category was identified by a humorous and meaningful code: "v" ("smiles" stood for emotion/positive acts); "." ("periods" stood for Bales' "gives" categories); "?" ("question marks" stood for Bales' "asks" categories); "^" ("frowns" stood for emotion/negative acts).

Codes were entered into a standard stenographer's notebook. The horizontal lines of the notebook became the time-order lines. Codes were entered top to bottom near the left hand margin. Square or triangular symbols written to the left of each code indicated the identification of the group initiating the interaction. For example, "triangle ?" would be used to code a triangle asking if the squares would be willing to change Rule 4. Using this system, longhand notes on rule changes and collective action could be written on the next time line. They were interspersed among Bales codes as necessary. Notes on rules changes were made by copying changes on the chalkboard *verbatim* into the notebook. Collective action notes began as soon as players left (or moved) their seats. These notes were taken in a manner similar to the way in which a journalist would record what she sees.

During pretesting a tape recorder was used to gather information on group interaction. Recordings of several pretest plays showed that the quality of the recording was barely acceptable even though the recorder was a good one. It picked up lots of noise such as that from the ventilation system, chairs being moved, and chalk as it squeaked on the chalkboard. The voice information contained on the recordings was difficult to understand, let alone to code. Also, if the recorder was used surreptitiously, ethical problems arose, but if players knew the recorder was being used, the play spirit was jeopardized. Because of these problems, tape recording was abandoned for both ethical and practical reasons. A human observer worked out much better than the machine. He sat in plain sight of everyone, quietly taking notes, and reminding everyone that "squares make the rules" whenever he was asked to clarify something. The observer became a learning resource during the debriefing because he could recount in detail who said what and what happened. Without exception, players seemed to be amazed at the accuracy and completeness of this information.

During pretesting, interobserver reliability of the modified Bales coding scheme was checked by looking at the percentages of codes in each of the categories. This procedure was recommended by Bales. No statistics were computed because the percentages in each category varied by four points or less between the two observers. In a separate analysis (also recommended by Bales) the time-ordered sequence of codes was checked. Over eighty percent of the codes matched. The single biggest problem seemed to be the identification of a "verbal act." Sometimes one observer would code an intergroup communication as two acts, while the other defined it as one. Following Bales, an "act" was defined as an "uninterrupted utterance." A second problem was that sometimes it was difficult to tell if a communication was meant for one's own group, for the other group, or for both. A decision was made that if the context of the communication did not limit it to one's own group, and if it could reasonably have been heard by the other group, it was to be considered an intergroup communication. Even before these clarifications were made, the coding of the interaction was well within acceptable limits as defined by Bales.

In retrospect, some earlier problems stemmed from the fact that "small groups" in the game behaved like the larger ones which they were supposed to represent, so small group methods had to be modified for use with them. In fact, after the first few plays, the author began observing verbal interactions and collective action for both groups, no matter which one was assigned to him. This process evolved naturally, as he watched the whole game. The other observer also evolved a method of notetaking whereby she began recording information on the content of communication as well as its process. During particularly interesting sequences, she took notes on both groups too. This system became so successful that in later plays the observer recorded most of the interactions within the group as well as all of the interaction between groups. Also, the observer recorded most of the content of these interactions. This additional information proved to be a great aid in understanding play. Some of the best examples of these observations appear in Chapter Eight.

Due to the vigor with which data were gathered immediately after the pretesting, the two sets of notes (from the observer and the administrator/ observer) were not compared until after a few games had been played. It came as a pleasant surprise that the notebooks matched each other almost exactly. This finding really provided the impetus for the later use of a single administrator/ observer.

COLLECTIVE ACTION

About one-third of the way through the data gathering, it became apparent that the verbal descriptions of collective action needed to be written in a more standard format, so the description of collective action from each play was transcribed onto a 3 x 5 inch card. These cards had no identification as agrarian or industrial versions of the game. The descriptions were ranked on the severity of collective action. A number of reliability checks yielded Spearman's Rhos of up to .96, but even though the statistics were well above acceptable levels, the dimension(s) behind the rankings did not seem clear--perhaps because the actions in the game are analogies to what might happen in the real world. Therefore, a coding scheme was needed that could be used with the game and in the real world. Studies by Bwy (1968) and by Russell (1974) provided a set of dimensions of collective action that was used in this research. In subsequent plays this coding scheme was incorporated into the initial written observations of collective action. The dimensions included the number of players who were involved in the collective action, the time it began, the time it ended, and the degree to which it was illegal.

DEBRIEFING

After play was completed, estimates of motility were made by players and the administrator. Then the post-game questionnaire items were completed. Finally, players were asked to replace all materials in the envelopes and to return them to the game administrator. Chairs were arranged into their original positions. Debriefing was begun by asking students if they had any questions about the game. Next, the administrator explained the meaning of each of the rules. The two types of society were explained. The discussion was tailored to lectures, readings, and to other class topics. Debriefing was an important part of the research design, too. During this time the administrator asked questions about the meanings of any game behaviors which seemed unclear. After the debriefing, observers went over their notes. Ambiguous codes were clarified, and the observers tried to come to an understanding on the *meaning* of major actions by the players.

SUMMARY

Any methodology represents an accommodation between the appropriate scientific canons, the theory to be tested, and the daily decisions which are required to execute the research. In research using gamed simulations, these concerns must be balanced against the requirement that a play spirit be maintained. In the research with STARPOWER much time and effort was expended in the maintenance of this delicate balance. Particularly in research with gamed simulations, the decisions concerning methodology need to be made explicit because the requirements of research with gamed simulation are different from those in the better-known types of research such as the laboratory experiment, the social survey, and the case study.

CHAPTER EIGHT

QUALITATIVE ANALYSIS
OF STARPOWER

The ideal role for the researcher in a gamed simulation is that of a *quantitative field worker*, and as such, the understanding of the game from the perspectives of the players is the most important goal of research. Since these perspectives develop as play progresses, subsequent quantitative data analysis necessarily must follow them. In order to place this discussion in the frame of reference of a player, observations by a fictitious player are presented below.

THE DAY WE PLAYED STARPOWER:
OBSERVATIONS BY A FICTITIOUS PLAYER

The day we played STARPOWER began like any other class day. We came into the classroom and noticed that all the seats had been arranged into two large circular groupings. I sat about where I usually did. The guest stopped writing on the chalkboard. He told us not to get too comfortable because we might have to move to another seat in order to start the game. He said we were going to play a game that our teacher told us about during our last class meeting. I asked myself, "Why would we move?" Everyone got a white envelope with some stuff in it. What was that? Put the tag on? Don't show the chips? Okay. My tag was in the shape of a triangle with the letters "AB" on it. My neighbor's tag was in the shape of a square. The guest told students wearing the triangular tags to move to the other set of seats, so we did. My neighbor stayed where she was, and other students wearing the square tags joined her. In the new set of chairs, everyone had different letters on their triangular badges. I thought, "This must be a group or something." Everyone was looking into their envelopes. We checked to make sure we had five chips. We did. I wondered, "Why can't we show them?" No lecture today. What's this game about? The guest finished writing on the board. The colors of the chips meant something. Yellow chips were the highest. I thought, "I don't have any. Five of the same color give you a bonus--ha, just like poker." Someone next to me was snickering. Everyone was seated now. A few students were still trying to pin on their tags.

We were told that the game was called STARPOWER, a game of trading and bargaining. I said to myself, "Yes, I'm going to try to get

111

over the values of each of the colors of the chips. I had three reds and two blues. I thought, "I need some yellow ones. One yellow is worth more than all five of my chips! Wait--the bonus for five of a color is worth twenty-five. Maybe I should go for five red ones. Each trade is worth twenty-five points. Maybe I don't need yellows after all. Look! To trade you have to hold hands with another player [laughter]." I saw some other rules on trades. I said to myself, "This sounds complicated. Hey, if I don't want to trade, I can fold my arms!" My teacher is making an arms-folded gesture [more laughter]. Next, I heard something about expelling someone. I promised myself, "I'll figure out what it means later."

Next we looked at scoresheets. I saw lots of boxes. The administrator talked about the top sheet. I thought, "OK, I see. Some boxes are for chips, and some are for bonuses. This looks like work!" I wrote my tag number in one of the boxes. Next, the administrator told us something about the timer. Someone in the other group asked, "Do we have to keep sitting?" I thought that the administrator just had told us that we could move around. Being noticeably patient, he told us that we could trade with anyone else. I thought, "The square group too! Great. Walking around will be fun." Now someone asked the administrator how to trade. He demonstrated the procedure by walking over to the front row and taking a girl's hand. He asked her if she had a red chip. Then he spoke for her and said, "yes." Then he offered her a white chip. The mock banter was kind of funny. It looked pretty easy.

Next, someone asked, "Why would she want to trade a red for a white?" He answered, "Maybe she was trying to earn bonus points." I replied to myself, "I hope that someone will give me a yellow one!" He said, "The best way to learn about a game is to play." Okay. The timer was set. People started to hold hands and bargain with each other. A person with a square tag approached me. She asked, "Will you trade?" I said, "Sure I'll trade." I took her hand and asked, "Got any yellows?"

-- A lower class player in an industrial version of STARPOWER

STARPOWER began with a trading round. After it was over, the score for each player was tallied on the chalkboard. These scores were the basis for a player's upward or downward motility. Trades in the game had something to do with scores. In order to understand trades as they were understood by players, answers to the question, "With whom did you trade?," are given by two fictitious *ideal-type* players. The first answer was given by a lower class player, a triangle, in an industrial society, and the second answer was given by an upper class player, a square, in an agrarian society.

With whom did you trade?

> I traded with players who looked like they might want to trade. I found out after a couple of trades that I wasn't going to get any yellow or green chips from other players, so I concentrated on making trades in order to earn the twenty-five point bonus. I found that it was just as profitable to trade with a square as with a triangle. I began trading with other triangles. After I traded with the most likely looking triangles, I began trading with some squares who wanted to trade. I made many trades with many different players in the game. When the scores were tallied on the chalkboard after the first round, I saw large differences among the players in our triangle group. Also, I noticed that several members of our group had scores that were higher than those of some members of the square group.
>
>> -- An answer given by an ideal-type triangle player in an industrial society

With whom did you trade?

> I traded with some fellow squares. I had collected two white chips toward the color bonus when this triangle engaged me in a trade. He wanted my yellow chip in exchange for a white or a red. I really wanted the white chip, but I wouldn't trade it for a yellow one. I said I'd give him my red one for the white, but he said, "no." We just stood there holding hands until the round was over. I know he was trying to get my valuable chip. I considered giving it to him just to get him off my back, but I decided that the 10 point bonus for three whites wasn't worth the loss of my yellow chip. When the scores were tallied on the chalkboard, I noticed that all of the scores of the triangles were really low. Our scores in the square group were high. No member of their group had a score which was higher than any of ours. Next round I'm going to go for three whites, but I'm only going to trade with fellow squares. When a triangle comes around, I'm going to fold my arms!
>
>> -- An answer given by an ideal-type square player in an agrarian society

GROUP BONUS

After the scores of players were tallied on the chalkboard, each social class was given three bonus chips that were worth twenty points each. The group could assign these chips to one or more of its members provided it could reach a unanimous decision on the recipient(s) within the three-minute time limit. Furthermore, the chips had to be in the possession of the recipient(s) when the timer signaled that time was up. The bonus points were added to the score of each recipient. A number of strategies were available to social classes in coming to their decision. Of particular interest is the fact that the bonus chips could help a player to gain upward motility, or they could prevent downward motility. Other strategies included helping to equalize scores in the group or rewarding the most successful members. In order to place these decisions in the frame of reference of players, two fictitious situations are described.

> The group bonus session took place after all of our scores were written on the chalkboard. The administrator placed three twenty-point bonus chips on the floor in the center of our group. He told us that we had three minutes to make a unanimous decision on which group members would receive them. If we couldn't decide, he would take them back. None of our triangle players had scores that were close to any of the squares, so we didn't even think about how the three bonus chips might move one of our players into the other group. Player "GH" suggested that the bonus chips be used to raise the scores of the three *lowest* triangles. All of us agreed. We felt good about our decision.
>
> -- An ideal-type triangle in an agrarian society
>
> We could see that several of the triangles had scores that were higher than the lowest members of our group. One of our members had such a low score that even all three twenty-point chips wouldn't help him, so we let him go. For our next two lowest scorers, the chips would make a difference, so we gave two bonus chips to player "34," and we gave one chip to "12." Later we found out that the triangles gave two chips to "HJ," their highest player, so our number "12" became a triangle after all. Anyway, at least we tried to save her.
>
> -- An ideal-type square in an industrial society

MOTILITY

After the group bonus session, scores for players were compared, and if the highest scoring lower class triangle had a score that was higher than that of the lowest square, the players traded places for the next round of the game. This situation is described by a fictitious player.

During the trading round, I made quite a few trades. It seemed more worthwhile to have fun and to make trades than to haggle endlessly over a deal that was going to earn only five extra points. After the round was over, I saw that with seven trades to my credit, I was the top scorer for the triangles. Then the group members gave me a twenty-point bonus chip. They said that I should try to "do something good" for them later on. On the chalkboard the game director drew a line which connected my identification letters, "FQ," with number "19," a member of the other group. The game director told me to switch places (and identification tags) with the player with whom I was paired by the chalkline. I'm now player "19," a square. I don't know how I can help the triangles, but I'm going to make lots of trades so I don't become one of them again!

    -- An upwardly motile player in an industrial society

Following motility, all participants completed two questionnaire items on their scoresheets. Next, they were told that there was to be a second round of the game that was exactly like the first one. After this round they were told that before a third round of the game began, squares would be given the authority to make the rules. The impact of this revelation is described by a fictitious player.

From the very beginning of the game I had this notion that I should hang on to my yellow chip. It seemed just too valuable to let it go, so I never offered it in a trade. I used only my other four chips. This strategy put my score just about in the middle of the square group. When I found out that we were going to make the rules, I thought, "Very interesting!" I knew from the first round that I wanted to remain a square, so I made sure that I held on to the yellow chip during the second round. I folded my arms and refused to trade with anyone else. I want to make some rules which will insure that I don't have to become a triangle--ever.

    -- An ideal-type square in an agrarian society

RULE CHANGES

Giving squares complete authority to make the rules sometimes had a drastic effect on play. Seven societies (of the sixty-four in the data set) never progressed beyond this phase of the game. Four upper class square groups simply ended the game and declared themselves to be the winners (three of these four societies were of the agrarian type). In three other societies, the players never finished the game. In one of the games which did not progress into the third round, the upper class members did not want to finish it. They did not want to repress the other group completely, and they didn't want to give the triangles any chance of upward mobility, so they purposely dragged-out the rule change portion of the game until the class time was exhausted.

In another one of these societies, the lowest scoring upper class squares progressively purged the higher scoring minority players from the group by using the rule which said that, "A majority vote by a group can expel a member from that group." When time ran out, the purge was continuing into its third stage, and only seven of the original sixteen players remained in the group. The lowest four players were about to take a vote on the expulsion of the three highest scoring players, who had not yet been expelled from the square group!

In another society, the squares became internally deadlocked over rule changes, so they ended the game as a way out of their deadlock. Two of these last three societies were of the agrarian type. Apparently, upper class members in the agrarian type of society found it more difficult to maintain their privileged status and to keep the game going than did squares in industrial societies. This "difficulty" was expressed in the form of complete repression by ending the game, in dragging it out, or in internal difficulties such as deadlock or internal purge.

Examples of Rule Changes

Some of the other patterns of rule making were not as dramatic as complete repression or internal purge, but they were no less creative. Repression of some sort was the norm. Typically it was expressed in one of the trading rules, and often it extended privilege to the squares but denied it to the triangles. None of the rules was immune from discriminatory manipulation. Some of the more colorful statements made by actual players are presented below.

Trading Rules

Rule 1 stated that, "All chips must be hidden." In eleven plays it was eliminated, and when a new rule replaced it, the triangles were worse off than before the change. Some examples are:

> "All square chips must be hidden, but triangles [chips] must be shown and no lip [sic]."

> "All triangles chips must be exposed [sic]."

In one play, the replacement rule was combined with another change to yield a rule which gave individual squares unlimited latitude.

> "After showing square[s] your colors [of chips, the] square[s] will readjust the values for the chips any time during the round."

Rule 2 was not immune to change by squares. In its original form it stated that, "Players must hold hands to begin talking." This rule was eliminated in over one-quarter of the societies. When a new rule replaced it, discrimination against triangles was common. An example is:

"Triangles must hold hands [in order] to begin talking."

Rule 3 stated that, "Players must keep holding hands until a trade has been made." In over one-half of the societies, this rule was eliminated, and typically, triangle privileges were restricted. Examples of these restrictions included the following ones:

"Triangles must trade with [their] hands [held] behind their backs."

"Squares may cancel a transaction at any time."

"Squares can break out of a deal, but triangles can't."

"Players must keep holding hands until a trade has been made. If no trade is made, triangles must give [up] the most valuable chip in [their] envelope."

Rule 4 stated that, "Trades must be one chip for one chip." In over one-fourth of the societies, this rule was eliminated. Typically, the replacement rule allowed any number of chips to be exchanged. Occasionally this rule was used against the lower class players, as in the following examples.

"Triangles can trade only once."

"[Triangles must trade] One chip for as many [chips] as squares want."

Rule 5 stated that, "Chips of the same color cannot be traded for each other." Almost one-third of the time, this rule was eliminated. Typically, its replacement allowed trades for chips of the same color. For example,

"Chips of the same color can be traded to break a stalemate."

This rule was not spared a discriminatory twist,

"[Squares] can trade color for color. Triangles can't."

Rule 6 stated that, "Players may avoid trading by folding their arms." In almost one-third of the plays, this rule was eliminated. Often its replacement matched the now familiar pattern of differential treatment of triangles. Examples are:

"Triangles must trade with squares."

"Triangle players may not avoid trading by folding their arms."

"Triangles must trade on demand by a square."

The replacement of this rule seemed to stimulate the squares to move to a more general repression of the lower class triangles, as the following examples show.

"[Members of the] Triangle group must give chips on demand."

"Triangles must give squares what they ask for. Squares may avoid trading by folding their arms."

"Triangles have to [sic] trade with squares--higher chips for lower chips."

A further level of repression is shown by rules which made the triangles completely dependent on squares for trading.

"Triangles must trade with squares only."

"A triangle must trade with a square or not at all."

"Triangles cannot trade with each other--only with squares. Squares can trade with anyone.

Rule 7 stated that, "A majority vote by a group can expel a player from that group." This rule was eliminated in only about a half a dozen plays. As with the other Trading Rules, the rules that replaced it generally resulted in greater repression of the triangles.

"A majority vote of squares can expel any triangle from a group."

None of the changes in the Trading Rules resulted in a clear advantage for the lower class triangles. The most they could hope for was no change at all. It was quite common for squares to eliminate rules that pertained to hand holding, forced trades, one-for-one trades and trades for chips of dissimilar colors. Particularly in closed societies, these rules represented the only chance that triangles had to tie-up squares and to "force" a favorable trade. Oddly, the triangles seldom complained when these rules were eliminated. After all, the elimination of these rules made *intragroup* trading more convenient. Perhaps by this time in the game, the additional convenience outweighed the loss of being able to "tie up" a square.

Chip Values

In almost one-third of the plays, chip values were changed. Sometimes, the value of yellow chips was raised to as high as 150 points. However, it was common in the industrial societies to decrease the value of the yellow chips-- sometimes to as little as five points--thereby making achievement *through trading* even more important to one's social position. Red, white, or blue chips sometimes were increased in value to a maximum of eighty points. Rarely did these changes result in motility or in changes in the relative wealth of the two groups.

In about twenty percent of the societies, the color bonus was changed by the upper class squares, and in about one-third of these societies, rule changes in the color bonus favored the lower class triangles. Some examples of these changes are:

"5 of a color = 125"
"None of a color = 50"
"Full house (three chips of one
   color and two of another)= 20"
"A straight (one of each color) = 25"

Rarely did these changes have any effect on motility. In fact, the rules governing the color bonus were "safe" rules for squares to change, since the effect of the change on motility could be gauged more accurately by squares than could the effects of other rule changes. Typically, the slight advantage to triangles of a change in the chip values was cancelled by a discriminatory trading rule.

Trading Bonus

In the industrial societies, the bonus for each trade was twenty-five points, and in the agrarian societies, this bonus was one point. The value of this bonus was changed by squares in seven industrial societies and in five agrarian societies. In the agrarian societies, the value of the bonus always was *raised*, but it never was raised to more than five points. In the industrial societies, it was lowered in most cases. In one industrial society, the bonus stayed the same for triangles, but it was raised to seventy-five points for squares! In three societies, it was lowered to ten points. In two societies, it was eliminated, and in one society it was raised to fifty points.

Summary of Rule Changes

In only four of the sixty-four societies was the lower class triangle group in the same position (or better off) after the rule changes than they had been before the changes took place. Two of these societies were of the industrial type, and two were agrarian.

Generally speaking, giving the upper class squares complete authority to make rules was an advantage which they used to further their own class interests at the expense of the triangles. In industrial societies, sometimes squares closed down the previously open channels of mobility, and in agrarian societies, squares sometimes made rules which attempted to humiliate the triangles. Of course, all of these misdeeds were accomplished with a laugh, in the name of fun.

In the sixty-four plays of STARPOWER equality between triangles and squares in both opportunity and resources came about only twice. In each case both squares and triangles regarded the equality as the logical *end* of the game. They did not know how to proceed further. Either these games or the societies which they represent (or both) are structured so that the response repertoires of players do not include ways of handling this "ultimate difficulty!"

Verbal Interactions

During the rule changes, the classes interacted with each other. These interactions were recorded using the modified Bales (1950) IPA coding scheme that is collapsed into the four categories of positive emotions, declarative statements, questions, and negative emotions. During the rule change portion of the game, each verbal act was coded into one of the four categories. When possible, the actual statement was recorded in longhand in hopes of further exploring the social processes involved.

Content of Verbal Interactions

Some of the things which squares said are indicative of their arrogance. One square announced,

"Do the minority groups [sic, only one group] have any suggestions which we can ignore?"

Another square stated matter-of-factly,

"I don't even want to hear from you people!"

Another said,

"Why be fair? If we got [sic] power, let's get it all!"

The structure of the social class system was so much a part of the situation that often, triangles fully understood this arrogance. They could not "reframe" the situation as an unjust one (Gamson, Fireman, and Rytina, 1982: 124-126). Talking among themselves, triangles once said,

"It's not to their benefit to listen to us."

A triangle in another game said,

"They don't help us."

The reaction to this observation by another triangle in the same game was,

"They're not supposed to!"

Some squares were sympathetic to the triangles. Often, these squares had been triangles in previous rounds. In a few cases their motility had been due to triangle group bonus chips. One of these marginal squares told another,

"You should give them a chance--listen [to them]."

The other square revealed his method of social control of the triangles,

"We can listen then shut 'em down."

Triangles often saw that these "new" squares could not help due to their marginal status, or they would not help because they had been fully coopted by the squares. Members of one triangle group said,

"Yeah, remember the little people."

(Then to themselves) "He's become a true square."

(Then they asked the square) "What happened to your roots?"

Another one of these sequences was especially noteworthy.

Triangle: "May I ask [a question] out of a sense of social consciousness?"

New square: "No."

Triangle: "Remember we put you in there."

New square, partly tongue-in-cheek: "It's been so long [ago, that] I don't remember the little people I stepped on to get here!"

Another square said,

"I can hardly believe [that once] I was a triangle."

Several others said of their attempts to help the triangle group,

"I tried."

Of course, newer, more marginal squares could be expelled by the older ones, so sometimes these newcomers were severely limited in their ability to help the triangles. Triangles frequently thought that the newer squares should help them more than they did.

Sometimes the triangles threatened these individuals. One group said,

"You've messed up. We'll get you."

The new square replied,

"I'll see if I can help you."

Very infrequently, square groups did not discriminate against triangles, and later they seemed to be *sorry* they had missed an opportunity to abuse the triangles.

Square: "I'll give you a break."

Triangle: "Thanks a lot."

Square (later): "I know that we did wrong now. We won't give you a break again."

Most square groups were not responsive to anything the triangles did. A few square groups seemed to be responsive only to triangle anger or threats, i.e., divesting acts that were aimed at breaking the bonds of authority (Gamson, *et al.*, 1982: 109-113).

In one game, squares agreed with themselves that,

"We better leave it the way it is, or they'll get bent out of shape [sic]."

In another game, a verbal exchange between the two groups took place as follows:

Triangles: "You clean the toilet."

Squares: "We'll listen to you."

Triangles: "We ain't gonna abide by your rules!"

Squares: "Okay, we'll change a few things."

Triangles: "Take it [a discriminatory rule] off there [gesture toward the chalkboard] or we'll walk [out]."

One square group tried to combine equality with complete repression, as a means of social control. This almost contradictory combination was presented to triangles in the following way:

Squares: "We make the rules. We don't want to play, so accept the equality or we'll screw you. You'll lose either way."

Triangles: "We don't want to be equal. We want a chance to win." "We want a fighting chance."

Other triangle groups also expressed their frustration at the injustice. Many triangle groups also expressed feelings of hostility and solidarity. Typical comments to themselves and to the other group included these:

"They won't listen."

"Squares only deal with the trivial rules, not the important ones."

"Up your nose [sic]."

"Ya bunch of turkeys [sic]."

"[You] Elite snob."

"Talk about a close group, man, we're together."

"Revolt."

"They make 'em, we break 'em." [reference to rules]

"Let's boycott their group. We could refuse to trade."

"Organize and overthrow."

"We shall overcome."

"We're unionized."

"If we just keep trading back and forth, there's nothing they can do."

COLLECTIVE ACTION

Occasionally, collective action was severe enough that it brought the game to an end. In order to place collective action in the frame of reference of players, two fictitious ideal-type scenarios are presented below. In the first scenario, a lower class triangle from an agrarian society explains why the triangles revolted.

Why did we revolt?

Well, we did it because of the squares. We didn't have any valuable chips, and we couldn't get any from the squares by trading. Even when they would trade with us (which was rare in the second round) they wouldn't give up any valuable chips. We were really worried when we found out that they were going to get to make the rules for the next round of the game. Last round we tried to get our player "H" into their group by giving her all of our group bonus points, but they blocked us. Then, later, when they started making those awful rules, we knew we were in trouble. We couldn't win. We couldn't even become members of their group. In fact, they wouldn't even listen to us when we spoke to them. Then they took away our rights to trade with each other. Player "ZH" said, "Let's go get 'em!" Under his leadership, we pooled all of our chips and gave them to "G" for safekeeping. As soon as the triangles tried to start-up the game again, we went over to their side of the room and took their envelopes. As "ZH" said, "How were they going to stop us?" At first, the squares didn't even know what was happening. "H" and some others even erased the rules on the chalkboard! Needless to say, the squares never got the game going. They just sat there while we took over the game. It was clear that no one was going to trade any more, so the instructor suggested that we should return to our seats and discuss our group strategies, if any. Everyone agreed, so we did.

-- A triangle in an ideal type agrarian society

In four of the simulated societies, the collective action was severe enough that a third round of the game never was completed. All four of these societies were of the agrarian type. In one of these societies lower class triangles pooled all of their resources and gave them to a lower class member for safekeeping. When upper class members tried to initiate a third trading round, all the triangles (except the one holding the chips) immediately surrounded the group of chairs occupied by the upper class members. The triangles prevented any trades from taking place by shouting and by standing between prospective traders of the square group.

Another simulated society collapsed. All members of the lower class removed their identification tags and refused to play as triangles. Most of them surrounded the chalkboard on which upper class members busily were writing rule changes. The triangles loudly voiced their dissatisfaction with the way in which squares handled their roles. Upper class members then changed a few insignificant rules. Triangles continued to voice their dissatisfaction, and they began to write their own rules on another chalkboard. The squares quit the game.

In another society, the lower class triangles refused to obey any rules. They gave the squares all their chips, but then all of the triangles entered the upper class group of chairs. They interspersed themselves among the upper class squares and brought the game to a halt by shouting and debate. The exasperated squares threw up their hands and quit.

In yet another society, lower class triangles closed off access to their group by moving the chairs together in a tight circle. They refused to trade with the upper class squares or to obey the rules. Although triangles behaved almost identically in ten other societies, in this one instance, the squares quit the game. In none of these societies did the upper class squares declare themselves to be the winners.

A few lower class triangle groups tried to interfere with trading by the squares by grasping their hands and demanding their most valuable chip in trade. This action "tied-up" the squares and prevented them from moving freely about the classroom, but it did not bring the society to a halt.

Square Collective Action

Collective action by the *square* group during the third round was much less frequent than that among the triangles, but it did occur. In two instances the squares refused to trade with the triangles. In two other instances, squares were very aggressive toward triangles. In one case they ripped several triangles' envelopes in half. Two triangles ran from the classroom in order to avoid being "victimized."

Collective Action Summary

Many other instances of collective action were not as dramatic as the examples above. Often, the triangle groups simply ignored the squares, even though they did not refuse to trade with them. It was a fairly common strategy for triangles to break game rules by showing their chips to each other, by pooling them, or by violating the rules on colors or numbers of chips to be traded. These strategies didn't take long to plan. Someone would suggest a strategy, and others would agree to it immediately.

In about one-fourth of the societies, a mixture of collective and individual action was observed. Some players were trading, and others were not. In these games, refusals to trade were made on an individual basis. Some players traded exclusively within their groups, while others traded with members of the other group. In a number of societies, triangles at first ignored the squares or refused to trade with them on an individual basis. As the round progressed, trading slowly returned to patterns established in earlier rounds.

Individual Action

In a number of societies, the third round of the game was characterized by even more trading than before, and players traded equally with members of their own group as well as with members of the other group. A fictitious square explains what happened in his ideal-type society.

Why did we continue to play STARPOWER through the third round?

Well, as far as I can tell, no one considered *not* playing it. In the second round many players realized that trading was the key to membership in the square group. We went around the room making as many trades as we could. Some players even seemed to be making multiple trades with the same partner. They earned a lot of points. Once the scores of all players were tallied on the chalkboard, we knew that a number of our lesser-trading players were going to be replaced by the higher-trading triangles. We gave our group bonus chips to our three highest traders as a reward for individual performance. During the rule change portion of the game, player "21" in our group suggested the elimination of the trade bonus. Members of both groups told this person that everyone deserved a fighting chance, so the bonus was left in the game. In fact the triangles wanted to raise the trading bonus, to fifty points, so we did. No one in either group wanted to hold hands, so we got rid of that rule. The rule changes took only about two minutes. The squares seemed eager to begin the third round, so the timer was set for five minutes. Everyone went crazy! Players traded with each other as fast as they could. No one really cared whether their partners were triangles or squares. The chips were really flying! At the end of the round several triangles had more points than some of the squares. They would have become squares had the game continued. After we looked at our scores on the chalkboard, the administrator stopped the game, and we discussed our individual strategies.

-- An upper class square in an ideal-type industrial society

In about one-quarter of the societies, trading proceeded with about the same or more vigor as in the earlier rounds, and trading occurred without much regard to intragroup trades versus intergroup trades. In these societies, action continued on an individual basis. Collective action did not occur at all.

A few societies were characterized by apathy on the part of the triangles. They did not interact either with members of their own group or with members of the other group. They just sat quietly in their chairs and waited for the round to end.

The observations point to a highly emergent quality of the verbal interactions, the changes in the rules, and subsequent collective action. Nothing in the previous rounds of play has prepared either group for the tremendous potential for change that occurs when the upper class squares are given complete authority to make rules for the next round of the game. Writers such as Smelser (1962) and Gamson *et al.* (1982) have stressed this emergent quality of collective action. Even though the conditions favoring it are present, collective action may not take place.

COMMENTS BY PLAYERS

As was discussed above, seven societies ended during the rule making. Four societies ended due to collective action. Two additional societies ended due to time limit problems that were not related to class conflict. Players in fifty-one of the sixty-four simulated societies played a third round of the game. In some of these games, competition was expressed by an increase in individual trading compared to earlier rounds.

In about one-third of the games, players were asked to record what was going on, from their point of view, during the third round of the game. Completion of these responses was the last activity that players undertook before the debriefing. While this information was not gathered for all of the games, the information that was gathered gives insights into players' perceptions that are not tapped in any other way.

Particularly in industrial societies which remained open to mobility through individual effort, players continued to play primarily *as individuals*. One square characterized the competitiveness of these societies,

"You've got to work hard to bring home more bread [sic]."

In fact, the group orientation that was necessary for successful allocation of bonus chips in Round 2 could break down almost entirely in the third round of an industrial society. A square described this process.

"The attitudes of our group completely changed. We became intensely involved--striving for as many points as we could accumulate. The atmosphere became very competitive--even with each other."

Another square discussed the pressure associated with fear of downward mobility,

"[I] feel good [about being] in the top group. [But, I felt] more and more crowded and trapped; [I was] ready for desperate, unfair (but not cruel) moves at end."

Other squares said,

"I based my campaign on getting the best *for me* regardless of the best interests of the group."

"Everyone became more aggressive in the third round."

In many other societies, the squares felt threatened *as a group*, and frequently they responded with organized repression. Squares described their actions in the following ways,

"We were able to make sure that no triangles became squares. The triangles were thought of as a threat, and the squares were much more conscious of becoming triangles than triangles [were of] becoming squares."

The squares made the rules, and [they] really limited what the triangles could do. We made sure they couldn't get extra points and get any of their people here. We were really close to each other and had strong ties."

"There was definite hostility towards the triangles by the squares. No opinions or suggestions were accepted by the squares [that were] presented by the triangles. The squares did everything to enhance themselves and prevent triangles from advancing."

The last round pulled us intensely together so as not to lose any [members] of our group. Each person was willing to contribute to keep this "core," even if sneaky ways had to be employed."

"It meant alot [sic] for me to belong to the winning group. In the last round we knew we had them beat [sic] so we shut them out."

A number of triangles reacted to repression by the squares:

"It is very discouraging to be a triangle during the last two rounds. I had the feeling that I couldn't really advance, but on the other hand, during the last round I felt that I really didn't want to advance to become a square. I prefer being a triangle. The rules of the third game [sic, round] were so unfair. I'm sure they would be illegal in private enterprise."

". . . at one point I would have preferred being a square--but forget it--they are indecisive, boring and intolerable as leaders."

"I was feeling hostile, frustrated because I could not do anything to influence the round. So I quit. I was unwilling to offer any competition on the grounds that I thought the situation was unfair."

Even though a square group might decide to repress the triangles, sometimes it had to overcome a minority within itself to do so.

"During the rule changes the group was fairly well divided . . . Those who wanted to change the rules to give themselves (our group) an edge, versus those who wanted the rules to stay the same and stay ahead or win on our own skill."

"Most of the squares were trying to insure their dominance in the easiest possible way. A few of us wanted to preserve competition."

In at least one square group, the majority of players wanted to help the triangles. Several squares reacted against this move, after the triangles really did get ahead.

"In real life--don't think of the other group--If you give them an inch, they win."

"If this were 'for real,' we wouldn't have been so nice to the other group."

Even squares who fully participated in making sure the squares won the game often felt guilty about it after the game was over. Some of these squares constructed elaborate rationalizations in order to explain or justify their behavior.

"I think our group was definitely trying to remain superior by blocking all routes of advantages for the other group. I think of this strictly as a game, but in actuality, I would not want to do this to the minorities. I think that they have as much right to gain as we do. I also feel that had the other group been in the lead, they would have done practically the same things to us. (Do unto others before they do unto you!)"

More frequently, squares just seemed to feel bad that their group had missed an opportunity to try out a more idealistic social system. Some of the squares said,

"I did not feel comfortable taking advantage of the disadvantaged group."

"I had decided that the maximum number of trades yielded the maximum points. I began making as many trades as possible in our own group--this also gave the groups the most number of trade points. I felt very shocked when I realized that this is exactly how elitist groups operate and how quickly I was caught up in the desire to further along my group and give them as many points as possible. How much better it would be if the groups ended up near equal with cooperation."

In the third round, we squares became greedy and were bound and determined to stop them [i.e., the triangles] from advancing completely. What we should have done was to help them advance along with us."

In some societies triangles continued trying to gain as many points as possible. In fact, some lower class triangle groups continued this strategy even after repression by the squares. Also, some triangle groups organized themselves even when it seemed unnecessary. In one of these societies, only Rule 6, "Players may avoid trading by folding their arms," had been replaced. The new rule said, "Players must trade till [sic] the end of [the] round." Squares considered themselves to be very threatened by *individual* competition from triangles, and from within their own group--a wide open society.

The triangle group, however, organized to compete as a group within the rules. One triangle said,

"The life of the triangle group was being threatened. We therefore had to defend ourselves by thinking fast or out thinking the other group in an attempt to earn more points."

Especially in societies which began as industrial ones, triangle players had to abandon aspirations of upward mobility in order to mobilize for collective action. Often, part of this process involved criticizing the other group. Some of these triangles told us,

"At first I tried to achieve a high score . . . I tried to abide by the rules . . . At the end I was interested in my group as a whole. We were underdogs and needed as much organization [as] we could muster."

"Watching the 'squares' change the rules made the 'triangles' angry and discontent [sic]. They gave us no consideration--it was all in the best interests of the squares. We tried to organize among ourselves and make up some of our own rules whereby we could 'survive.' Everyone pulled together for the best interests of the group rather than the individual. We hate the other group--they're power hungry snobs! I wanted to be a square at first--now I wouldn't consider it."

"At first, I was out for myself, trying to get the most points for myself. I was forced to change to the losing group. I found myself again trying to make the most points for myself. After the other group made discriminating [sic] rules, my feelings changed. I was out to help my group as much as possible."

Triangle organization in industrial societies which remained open to upward mobility most often resulted in action *within* the rules.

"In the last round triangles really worked together. They thought of ways to get more trades to add up points which squares never thought of because they had the [high] score[s] to begin with."

"I think the triangles finally decided to help each other [to] increase individual scores. Up to this point we had a sense of competition or struggle for the individual. 'Everyone was out for themselves.'"

"My group worked together, we planned to keep out the other group and increase our score a great deal by mass trading."

Using a loophole in the rules, one triangle group developed cooperative trading into a highly profitable endeavor,

"In trading, we made a verbal agreement, since the rules did not state that the trades required physical exchange of the chips. In this way, we could trade chips alot [sic] faster. Since the other group didn't want to trade with us, we traded among ourselves."

Triangle groups, however, often reacted to square behavior by reframing repression by the squares as unjust and by organizing their group for collective action which departed from patterns established in earlier rounds of the game. The players often mentioned that a change took place in their *orientation* to play. They were quite creative in comparing game strategies with various types of collective action in the real world.

"If you feel that you are not receiving *equal opportunity*, you will break rules to come out on top--and even feel justified about it."

"At the beginning of the game we were all for ourselves. As the game went on and we knew what was happening . . . we as a group started to *rebel* against them."

"When we saw how the other groups were [sic] taking away our rights of equality we all knew we must stick together. So we traded among ourselves so none of us would go under. We kept each other *alive* when the others wanted to *kill* us."

"Triangles realized they couldn't profit at all under the new rules so they set up a *trade embargo* against the other group."

"We tried *isolationism* combined with maximum group cooperation for trading and bonuses."

"In the triangle group we realized that there was no way to reach the square group by reason or an appeal to humanitarian concern, so we all agreed to exclude their participation . . . [from] our efforts. We knew we would not any of us [sic] rise to their level, but within our group we could all benefit from mutual support. We didn't wind up rich, but we all gained a great deal of *wealth* and a feeling of solidarity with our own group. We more or less formed a *new society*."

Sometimes, the triangle groups were not completely organized, even though intense pressure was provided by repressive rules and by ingroup processes. A triangle in the same society which produced the quote immediately above, said,

"Part of our group was trying to preserve our highest members in fear of the other group. I more or less didn't get involved and did the best I could."

SUMMARY OF THE OBSERVATIONS

The observations provide an understanding of play from the points of view of the players. Such insights often are lost in quantitative data analysis like that in the next chapter. The autotelic nature of play is the keynote of the gaming technique, so the procedures which render gaming amenable to scientific study must not overwhelm the spirit of play. Observations by players and by game administrators seem to be an ideal technique for use with games.

Almost universally, repression of the lower class triangles emerged in the game. In sixty out of the sixty-four societies the lower class triangles were worse off after the changes in the rules than before them. The four societies in which the triangles were the same or better off after the changes are split evenly between the industrial and the agrarian types of societies.

The comments of the players highlighted the importance of square repressiveness in the game. The squares used the rule making authority to give themselves advantages which (from an objective point of view) they did not need. Their repressiveness was a clear challenge to the triangles to react *if they could*.

Many triangle groups organized during this part of the game. Triangle organization was hampered by difficulty in reframing the situation as one of injustice and by difficulty in developing a plan of action which actually *helped* the group. In agrarian societies and in those repressed by the squares' rules, the triangles were more likely to give up hope of advancing themselves within the rules, so they tried to punish the squares by refusing to trade with them.

In many societies, the triangles never really got organized as a group, and the third round was apt to be characterized by apathy, individual refusal to trade, or trading that was restricted to the individual level. There was no doubt that repressiveness affected the lower class triangles, but collective action demanded creativity, organization, and alacrity on the part of the triangles. There was only a short span of time during which aggressive action could be taken. If they couldn't respond collectively and immediately, the opportunity for collective action passed. Given these facts, perhaps a low level of predictability in the quantitative analysis in the next chapter is to be expected. Were researchers to intervene in the interaction process during the last portion of the game in order to gather more data, emergent qualities of the interaction would be altered, if not curtailed.

Eleven simulated societies underwent drastic change. In four societies, the upper class squares completely repressed the lower class triangles by ending the game. Three of these societies were of the agrarian type, and one was of the industrial type. Three simulated societies failed to continue because of the internal collapse of the upper class square group. Two of the societies were of the industrial type, and one was an agrarian-type society. Four societies were brought to a halt as a result of disruptive collective action by the lower class triangles. All four of these societies were of the agrarian type.

Fifteen simulated societies continued a pattern which was reflective of the second round of play. Eleven of those societies began as industrial societies, and four of them began as agrarian societies. Nineteen industrial societies and nineteen agrarian societies exhibited patterns which were midway between the extremes of drastic change and "business as usual."

Even in spite of repression in both types of societies, in those which begin with a low level of technological efficiency and ascriptive status (agrarian societies), more often groups were expected to be the agents of conflict, and collective action was more dramatic when it occurred. In societies which began with a higher level of technological efficiency and achieved status, individuals competed with each other. Even in spite of elite repression, collective action in these societies was apt to be directed at replacement of the upper class through mobility rather than through the game analogues of more violent conflict. These findings should hold true for both real societies and for their simulated counterparts.

CHAPTER NINE

FINDINGS FROM THE
QUANTITATIVE ANALYSIS OF
COLLECTIVE ACTION IN STARPOWER

The quantitative field worker encompasses the notion of "critical theory" in which one uses social science concepts to illuminate processes which are not seen readily by the participants. The role of quantitative field worker also encompasses the ethnographic approach in which the field worker attempts to understand action from the point of view of the participants. Finally, the quantitative field worker uses experimental designs, quantification, and statistical analysis to test models of the processes to be studied. Currently, social science research is characterized by an overreliance on just one of these methods, and as such, the understanding that is gained is limited. The unique attributes of gamed simulations lend themselves to the broader approach of quantitative field work. In this chapter a quantitative analysis of collective action in STARPOWER is presented.

ROUND 1
Social Structure
Three variables make up the block labelled "social structure." These variables are social class (lower = triangles and upper = squares), type of society (agrarian or industrial), and group size. The variables are independent of each other, and they are the main independent variables in the model.

Status Characteristics
Mobility (changes in wealth of a social class), inequality (variation in wealth within a social class), and motility (changes in social class membership) were combined to form a block called status characteristics. In order to form this block, each of the variables was put into standard score form. The variables then were added to each other to form the status characteristics block. Social structural variables were used to predict this block. Type of society was correlated .64 with the status characteristics block (see Figure 9-1). This finding means that 41 percent of the variation in the status characteristics of a group can be explained by the type of society (agrarian or industrial). This relationship was statistically significant beyond the .001 level. The effects of social class and group size on status characteristics were not statistically significant. In addition to the main statistical technique of multiple regression analysis, a separate analysis of variance was performed on the data in order to examine statistical interaction among the independent variables. In order to perform the anova, the variable of class size

136

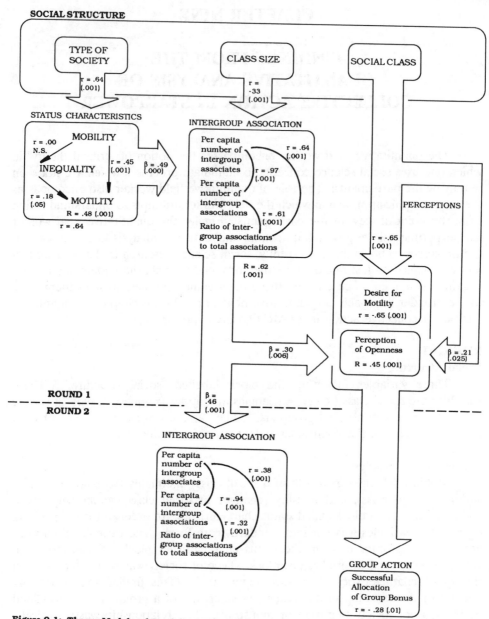

Figure 9-1: Theory Model and Statistical Test for Round 1

was dichotomized. Classes that were composed of five to nine players were considered to be small social classes, and those that were composed of ten to eighteen players were considered to be large social classes. No statistical interactions were observed among type of social class, type of society, or class size on status characteristics. Since social class and class size were not correlated with the type of society, statistical control of these independent variables was not necessary for the examination of the effect of type of society on status characteristics; therefore, betas are equal to the corresponding zero-order correlation coefficients. For the sake of simplicity, the correlation coefficients are presented where appropriate for all relationships. These findings mean that in the first round of the game, the type of society had an important effect upon changes in players' scores, variations in scores, and ultimately in player motility. The data supported Hypothesis 1-1a.

Relationships Within the
Status Characteristics Block

Examination of zero-order correlation coefficients between the type of society (agrarian vs. industrial) and the variables of the status block (coefficients not shown) reveals that, as expected, far more mobility and motility took place in the industrial version than in the agrarian version of the game.

Unlike Blau's predictions the degree of inequality was not correlated with the amount of mobility ($r = .00$). Derived from the Blau model is a finding that as the mobility of a social class increased, so did its rate of motility ($r = .45$). As predicted by the Blau model, inequality and motility were related statistically, but this relationship was weak ($r = .18$; $p = .05$). Hypothesis 1-1b was partially supported by the data.

The multiple correlation coefficient for the prediction of motility of $R = .48$ meant that twenty-three percent of the variation in motility was explained by variation in the linear additive combination of mobility and inequality. The average amount of change in scores within a game group (mobility) was more predictive of the movement of players from one group to another ($r = .45$; $p < .001$) than was the distribution of scores among the players of a group (inequality). Generally speaking, this finding meant that in STARPOWER the amount of resources which come into a group through trading was evenly distributed among players so that inequality is not affected.

Intergroup Association
In Round 1

Blau saw the pattern of intergroup association as being the most important characteristic of a social system, since it was a reflection of the integration of the system. He looked at the structure of the society as the main influence on intergroup association. Three main indicators of intergroup association discussed by Blau were used in this research: per capita number of intergroup associates, per capita number of intergroup associations, and the ratio of intergroup associations to total associations.

Since each of these variables was a slightly different measure of the extent of intergroup association, the variables were conceptualized to be interrelated with each other, but this interrelation was not assumed to be causal. Empirically, the variables were highly interrelated. Correlation coefficients showing this interrelationship exceeded .6, and all coefficients were statistically significant beyond the .001 level. The data supported Hypothesis 1-2a.

In order to form the block of "Intergroup Association," each of the three measures was converted to a standard score. These scores were added to each other to obtain the value for the block. Both class size and status characteristics were predicted to affect the amount of association that a social class would undertake with the other class in its society.

The Effect of Social Structure
On Intergroup Association

The social structural variable of class size affected the amount of intergroup association. As class size increased by one standard deviation, the association block decreased .33 standard deviation. This relationship was statistically significant beyond the .001 level. The direction of this relationship is opposite to that predicted by Blau. Evidently, since players were physically closer to members of their own group, they tended to associate with ingroup members first. Only when they had explored these ingroup possibilities did they investigate associations outside of their group. In the limited time of the trading rounds, players in larger groups did not exhaust the ingroup possibilities, so the larger was the size of the group, the *less* was the intergroup association. Hypothesis 1-2b was not supported by the data, but a relationship existed between class size and intergroup association. It was opposite in direction to the prediction.

Incidentally, intergroup association was not affected by social class. Also, it was not affected by the type of society (after status characteristics were taken into account statistically). Finally, no statistical interactions were observed for the effects of type of society, social class and class size on intergroup association.

The Effect of Status Characteristics
On Intergroup Association

As status characteristics increased by one standard deviation, intergroup association increased by .49 standard deviation. A relationship between type of social structure and intergroup association would be expected as an artifact of the "dogleg" relationship between type of social structure, status characteristics, and intergroup association (see Davis, 1975). Analysis of the betas showed that the relationship between type of society and patterns of association vanished when status characteristics entered the regression equation. The data supported the model in general and Hypothesis 1-3 in particular.

Additive Effects of Group
Size And Status Characteristics
On Intergroup Association

The multiple correlation coefficient, R = .62, meant that thirty-eight percent of the variation in intergroup association was explained by variation in the linear additive combination of class size and the status characteristics of a social class. This relationship was statistically significant beyond the .001 level. The optimum conditions for high intergroup association were a high rate of mobility/inequality/motility and small class size.

Perceptions

Perceptions and attitudes by social classes are conceptualized as resulting from the interactions of their members. Two measures of perceptions are desire for motility and perception of openness of the social system. Since there was no strong theoretical rationale for combining them, and since the two measures were not correlated highly ($r = .06$), they were treated as separate dependent variables in the analysis.

Desire for Motility

The desire for motility on the part of a social class depended upon which group it chose as a reference group. Until a lower class developed its own organization, its members were more likely to identify upward, and upper classes were apt to be characterized by members who identified with their own group. In fact, social class proved to be the only non-zero predictor of desire for motility. The zero-order correlation of -.65 ($p < .001$), when it was squared, indicated that 40 percent of the variation of desire for motility of the groups was explained by the social class of the group. Lower class groups tended to be made up of players who wanted motility, and upper class groups did not. The data supported Hypothesis 1-3a, but they did not support Hypothesis 1-3b.

Perception of Openness

The perception of openness of a social system by classes of participants within it was predicted to be influenced mostly by social class, interaction patterns, and perhaps by status characteristics. However, this last relation should have been an artifact of the presumed causal relations between status characteristics and intergroup association, on the one hand, and between intergroup association and perception of openness on the other. As expected, each of these three predictors was correlated with the perception of openness of the social structure, and as predicted, the pattern of partials revealed that only social class (Beta = -.21, $p < .03$) and intergroup association (Beta = .30, $p < .006$) had independent effects upon perception of openness. Intergroup association had the stronger effect. As it increased by one standard deviation, perception of openness increased by .3 standard deviation. The frequency with which players traded with members of the other class evidently affected their perceptions about the possibility of lower class members becoming upwardly mobile if they chose to do so.

Contrary to the prediction above, lower class members actually perceived the social class system as more open than did members of the upper class (Beta = -.21). Perhaps a greater desire for motility on the part of the lower class ($r = -.65$) created a perception of the possibility of motility. The multiple correlation coefficient (R = .45, p < .001), when it was squared, indicated that 20 percent of the variation in perception of openness was explained by the linear additive combination of social class and intergroup association. The data did not support Hypothesis 1-3c, but there was a relation between social class and perception of openness. It was in the direction opposite to that predicted by the hypothesis. The data supported Hypothesis 1-3d.

Group Organization and Action (not shown)

The ability of a group to undertake coordinated action was predicted to be related inversely to its degree of intergroup association, and upper classes should have had a less difficult time in taking group action than lower classes. None of the components of the model for Round 1 was predictive of successful allocation of the group bonus chips. Since the success of the decision on the chips was dependent on the group reaching consensus quickly, any thoughtful discussion decreased the chances of successful allocation, so predictability broke down. The single variable of inequality within a class was related weakly (r = -.15 p < .06) to successful allocation.

As the spread of scores increased within a class, players faced a more complex decision. Should they reward the players who already were successful? Should they award the chips to the lowest-scoring players in an effort to even-out the scores within the group? The bonus chips could affect motility of players, but they could not substantially blunt the inequality, so any discussion involving the decrease in inequality of the scores within a group could become quite involved, thus increasing the chances of the group losing the chips through indecision. The data supported neither Hypothesis 4-1a nor 4-1b.

Summary

The data analysis for Round 1 supported a theoretical model which gave an integral place to social structure, status, associational patterns, and perceptions in the understanding of play within the simulated societies generated by STARPOWER. In several instances, the directions of relationships were different from what the model predicted. These findings suggested that more attention be paid to conditions under which additional resources coming into a group will not affect the distribution of resources within it. Also, attention should be paid to proximity relationships (who sits next to whom), for in the short run, larger groups offer more opportunity for exchange within the group than outside of it.

In the game, the societies operated as expected. For instance, agrarian societies were characterized by lower mobility, lower within-class inequality, and lower motility. These status characteristics in turn affected intergroup association. In Blau's terms, agrarian societies were characterized by less integration.

ROUND 2
Social Structure and
Status Characteristics

Social structure in Round 2 was conceptualized in the same way as it was in the previous round; therefore, predictions were the same as they were in Round 1 (see Figure 9-2). The same variables made up the block on status characteristics as were used in the previous analysis; however, in this round two additional predictors of status characteristics were considered, even though they were not cast

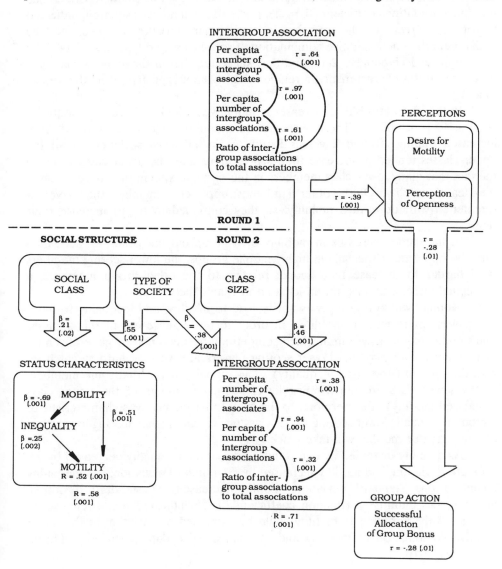

Figure 9-2: Diagram of Theory Model and Statistical Test for Round 2

as hypotheses. Status characteristics from Round 1 might have influenced the characteristics in Round 2. Associational patterns or perceptions also might have influenced the status characteristics in Round 2.

The pattern of partials indicated that social class and type of society were the only predictors which exhibited independent effects on status characteristics in Round 2. The difference in social class between groups accounted for .21 standard deviation change in status characteristics. The difference in type of society accounted for .55 standard deviation increase in status characteristics. The multiple correlation coefficient ($R = .58$, $p < .001$), when it was squared, indicated that thirty percent of the variation in status characteristics was explained by variation in the linear additive combination of social class and type of society. The data supported Hypothesis 2-1a, and they suggested that in the game, social class influenced status characteristics, a relation that was not expected in the theoretical model.

Within the status block, increases in mobility resulted in decreased inequality ($r = -.69$, $p < .001$). These increases in mobility could have resulted from increased trading (Round 2 versus Round 1) in industrial societies. Also the upper classes tended to increase their scores more than did lower classes due to the fact that many lower class members in the agrarian system may have rejected the idea of mobility. On the other hand, most upper class members may have felt threatened with downward mobility, so they continued to try to increase their score.

In the game, increases in mobility by a group did not generate inequality--just the opposite. Especially in highly mobile groups, the lower-scoring members tried harder to increase their scores relative to the other group members, a contextual effect that was not anticipated in Blau's theory.

Mobility within a group was apt to lead to motility, and inequality within a group was apt to lead to motility. In order to make sense out of this analysis, one should imagine a system in which competition between players generates a lot of mobility for all players. Lower scoring players are working hard to catch up with their group (decreased inequality). This mobility means that some members of the lower class are outstripping lower scoring members of the upper class (increased motility). Furthermore, to the extent that inequality is characteristic of a group (especially lower scoring upper class players and higher scoring lower class players) greater motility will take place.

As mobility increased by one standard deviation, inequality decreased by .69 standard deviation, and motility increased by .51 standard deviation. As inequality increased one standard deviation, motility increased .51 standard deviation. Squaring the multiple correlation coefficient of .52 indicated that twenty-seven percent of the variation in motility could be explained by variation in the linear additive combination of mobility and inequality. The data partially supported Hypothesis 2-1b.

Patterns of Intergroup
Association

The interrelation of the three separate measures of intergroup association broke down somewhat by Round 2. The number of players with whom one traded and the number of trades which were made still were highly intercorrelated, but higher numbers of these associations did not raise the ratio of intergroup associations to total associations. Groups characterized by high levels of association made considerable numbers of trades both within and outside of their own groups.

The strongest predictor of intergroup association in Round 2 was the pattern of intergroup association from the first round (Beta = .46, p < .001). Evidently, the actual process of play on an interpersonal level, as measured by this variable, was the most important predictor of subsequent associational patterns.

In the prediction of intergroup association in Round 2, status characteristics again were considered. A zero-order correlation of .31 (.001) was observed between the block of status characteristics and intergroup association. This relationship vanished when other variables were controlled statistically.

As in the first round, the type of society had an important effect upon status characteristics (Beta = .55, p < .001; discussed above). It also had an effect upon intergroup association (Beta = .38, p < .001). The type of society helped players to define their *potential* relations with each other. On the other hand, the intergroup associations *are* the measures of the actual relationships.

The beta for the relationship between status characteristics and intergroup association was .06 (N.S.). Before the controls were introduced, the zero-order correlation between these variables had been .31. The fact that the relationship vanished when other, prior variables were controlled, led to the deduction that the type of society in Round 2 was an explanatory variable that influenced both status characteristics and intergroup association. Statistically the relationship between status and intergroup association was an artifact of the relationship between social structure and status on the one hand, and social structure and association on the other. Perhaps in Round 2, players realized more fully the potential effects of social structure both for mobility and for associational patterns.

Reexamination of data for Round 1 showed that status was an intervening variable between the type of social structure and intergroup association. The zero order correlation coefficient between type of social structure and intergroup association was .38. The beta became .05 between the two variables when status was controlled. Evidently, as players gained more experience with the game through play, the effects of type of society in the prediction of intergroup association became more direct and more independent of status characteristics (scoring). Players saw the possibilities allowed by trading with the other group, and they acted upon them.

As discussed above, the most important predictors of intergroup association in Round 2 were the patterns that were established in the first round. As intergroup associational patterns in Round 1 increased by one standard deviation, intergroup associational patterns in Round 2 increased by .46 standard deviation (status characteristics and type of society were controlled statistically).

As the type of society changed from agrarian to industrial, intergroup association increased .38 standard deviation. The square of the multiple correlation coefficient (R = .71, p < .001) meant that fifty percent of the variation in associational patterns was explained by the linear additive combination of earlier patterns of intergroup association and by the type of society. No statistical interaction was observed among type of society, social class, and class size on intergroup association. The data supported Hypothesis 2-2a and 2-2d. They did not support either Hypothesis 2-2b or 2-2c. The analysis suggested that type of society had a direct effect on intergroup association and that previous associational patterns affected intergroup association. Intergroup association was highly predictable from variables in the model even though specific hypotheses were not supported.

Group Organization
And Action

In Round 2, the groups again had an opportunity to take action in the allocation of group bonus chips. In the first round, successful allocation could not be predicted by the variables in the model. However, by Round 2, the model contained the predictors of perception of openness of the social system, and desire for motility. Both variables were measured at the end of Round 1.

The individual effects of these two predictors were small, so for the sake of simplicity, the two independent variables were added to each other to form a block, even though their intercorrelation was low (.01). The correlation between this block, called "perceptions," and the successful allocation of the group bonus chips was -.28 (p < .02).

The strength of this relationship may have been depressed by the fact that the successful allocation of the bonus chips was an easier task in Round 2 than it was in Round 1 because the groups already had practiced it earlier in the game. Ninety percent of all groups successfully allocated the chips. As a device in the game, the group bonus session encouraged groups to organize, and it allowed them to have a success in taking action as a group. The data did not support either Hypothesis 2-3a or 2-3b. They did support Hypothesis 2-3c and 2-3d.

TRANSITION PERIOD AT
THE END OF ROUND 2

Immediately after motile players changed groups, the idea was made clear to players that the squares would make the rules for Round 3. At this time all participants were asked to complete about a dozen questionnaire items on play of the game (see Figure 9-3).

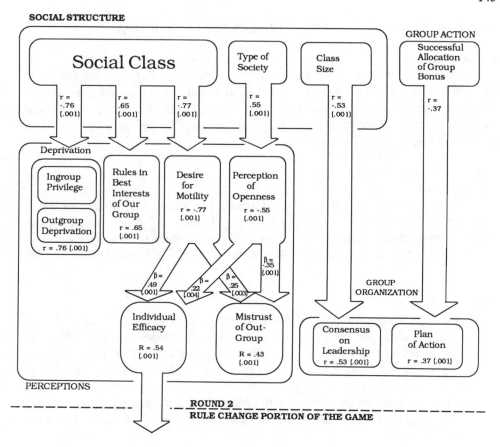

Figure 9-3: Diagram of Theory Model and Statistical Test for the End of Round 2

Perceptions

The theoretical model predicted that social structure would have an effect upon a set of perceptions concerning play. These perceptions included variables such as the following ones: 1) feelings of privilege and deprivation, 2) the extent to which game rules favored one social class over the other one, 3) the collective desire for motility by a class, 4) the perceptions of openness of the social structure by a class, 5) perceptions of consensus on leadership and perceptions of having a plan of action by a social class. These perceptions referred to play. They did not concern directly the evaluations of the other group. Another set of variables contained an aggregate measure of efficacy and a measure of mistrust of the other group. These measures are attitudes, as defined in Chapter Three.

Partial correlation analysis (not shown) revealed that the perceptions form intervening links between social structure and attitudes. The data do not support the notion of direct effects of social structure upon these attitudes.

Deprivation

Fifty-eight percent of the variation ($r = -.76$, $p < .001$) in deprivation was explained by social class. Once it became clear to players that upper class players would receive complete authority to make the rules of the game, social class became a primary predictor of perceptions of play in the game. The data supported Hypotheses 2-4a and 2-4b.

Rules in the Best Interests
Of Our Group

Social class should have become a strong predictor of the extent to which rules were perceived as favoring one's group. Indeed, forty-two percent of the variation in the perception of rules being in the best interests of one's group was explained by class differences ($r = .65$, $p < .001$). The data supported Hypothesis 2-4c.

Desire for Motility

Social class strongly affected desire for motility, as in the first round, but in Round 2, fifty-nine percent ($r = .77$, $p < .001$) of the desire for motility was explained by social class. Generally, lower class members wanted to gain access to the upper classes, and upper class members wanted to maintain their upper class status. At this point in the game, the majority of the members of even the most organized triangle groups would not have chosen to remain in their groups if they were given an opportunity to be upwardly motile. The data supported Hypothesis 2-4d.

Openness

The type of society was a strong predictor ($r = .55$, $p < .001$) of perceptions of openness. Players perceived correctly that it was the rules that affected mobility. In the first round, social class and intergroup association were the primary predictors of openness, and of the two variables, intergroup association had the stronger effect. Players' interactions were the bases of the formation of perceptions. By Round 2, players had moved up cognitively to a greater level of generality in their understanding of the game, and therefore, the prediction of the perception of openness was even stronger. Now thirty percent of the variance (versus twenty percent in Round 1) in perception of openness was explained by the type of society.

Incidentally, the pattern of partials (not shown) indicated that the zero order correlation between intergroup association and openness ($r = .37$) vanished when type of society was controlled statistically. The observed relationship was an artifact of the relationships between type of society and intergroup associations (discussed above) and between type of society and openness. The type of society *explained* the relationship between intergroup association and openness. The data supported Hypothesis 2-4e.

Efficacy

The extent to which a class was made up of individuals who desired motility and who believed the social class system to be open, the class was characterized by an attitude of efficacy. The pattern of partials indicated that desire for motility was an intervening variable between social class and individual efficacy. Lower class groups were most desirous of motility ($r = -.77$, discussed above). Groups that desired motility were most likely to feel efficacious (beta $= .49$, $p < .001$). Also, the pattern of partials revealed that perception of openness was an intervening variable between type of society and individual efficacy. Groups in industrial societies were likely to perceive the openness ($r = .55$), and groups that perceived greater openness in motility channels were more likely to be made up of members who felt efficacious as individuals (beta $= .22$, $p < .004$). The data did not support Hypotheses 2-5a and 2-5b.

As the desire for motility increased by one standard deviation, efficacy increased by .49 standard deviation. As perception of openness increased by one standard deviation, efficacy increased by .22 standard deviation. The square of the multiple correlation coefficient of .54 showed that twenty-nine percent of the variation in individual efficacy was explained by variation in the linear, additive combination of desire for mobility and perception of openness.

According to the model, social class had an effect on desire for motility, and type of society had an effect on perceptions of the simulated social structure (perception of openness). These variables, in turn, affected the degree to which players felt that they could influence others in the game. Put another way, to the extent that a player wanted to be a member of the other group and felt that he could do so, he also felt that he could have an effect on members of the group to which he aspired. Since from previous analyses, he was likely to interact with them (intergroup association), this perception seemed to be warranted. The data supported Hypotheses 2-5c and 2-5d.

Mistrust

Mistrust of a group by individuals of another group in STARPOWER could be predicted by two variables in the model. As individuals in a group were less desirous of motility, they began to consolidate as a group. The pattern of partials (not shown) revealed that desire for motility was an intervening variable between social class and mistrust. Upper class members did not want to move down ($r = -.77$ $p < .001$). Furthermore, they did not want the group to lose members through motility. They felt threatened (both personally and on behalf of the group) by the idea that lower class members could move up.

Also, lower class members generally desired motility ($r = -.77$), but it was likely that they perceived that the upper class members had an interest in maintaining their own positions; thus these squares would try to block upward motility. Their own desire for mobility helped triangles to emphasize for themselves just how fragile were their chances of upward mobility, given the fact that squares would be making new game rules before the next round of the game (beta = .25, p < .003).

The pattern of partials (not shown) revealed that perception of openness was an intervening variable between type of society and mistrust. In an industrial society individuals tended to perceive the class system as having open channels of motility (r = .55 p< .001). Furthermore, as a society had open channels of motility, there tended to be more actual movement of individuals (motility). The membership of these groups was changing constantly, and players of a group had less reason to trust a group with a shifting constituency (beta = -.35 p <.001), than they had to trust one with a more stable, predictable membership. Lower class members desired motility much more than did members of the upper class (r = -.77). Desire for motility put players in a situation of individual competition with other players. This competition was especially keen with members of the other class, so players tended to mistrust them. As desire for motility increased by one standard deviation, mistrust increased by .25 standard deviation (beta = .25, p < .003).

Perception of openness was more characteristic of industrial than of agrarian societies, as would be expected. A greater perception of openness was reflective of an achievement orientation in which those who worked the hardest earned the most points legitimately; therefore, perceptions of greater openness resulted in less mistrust of the other group. As openness increased by one standard deviation, mistrust decreased by .35 standard deviation (beta = .25, p < .003). The data did not support Hypotheses 2-5e and 2-5f, but they did support Hypotheses 2-5g and 2-5h.

Group Organization:
Consensus on Leadership

Two major aspects of group organization which came up in the theoretical analysis in Chapter Three were the development of consensus on leadership and the development of a plan of action. For the sake of clarity these two components of group organization were analyzed separately.

As predicted, larger groups were proportionally harder to organize. Within them, consensus on the emergence of occupants of leadership roles became increasingly difficult as they grew in size. Twenty-eight percent of the variation in consensus in leadership was explained by group size (r = .53, p < .001). The data did not support Hypothesis 2-6a or Hypothesis 2-6c, but the data did support Hypothesis 2-6b.

Plan of Action

The strongest predictor of perceptions by a class as having a plan of action was the successful allocation of the group bonus chips in Round 2. Fourteen percent of the variation in perception of having a plan of action by a group was explained by prior successful allocation of group bonus chips ($r = .37$, $p < .001$). The data did not support Hypothesis 2-6d or 2-6e, but they did support Hypothesis 2-6f.

Summary of the Transition
Period at the End of Round 2

The analysis in this section showed that the variables of social class and type of society were the primary predictors of perceptions of play and perceptions. In turn, these perceptions were the most effective predictors of the attitudes of individual efficacy and mistrust of the other group in the game.

Also in this section, the social structural variable of group size was shown to affect group leadership, and previous group action was shown to affect perceptions of a group having a plan of action. Consensus on leadership and plan of action will be among the most important predictors of group behavior to be considered in the next section.

RULE CHANGES

The dependent variables are the number of rule changes that were made by upper class members and the repressiveness of new rules. Since squares had the exclusive right to make rules, the variable of social class was not part of this analysis.

For the first time in the game, the two classes which made up each society had functional differences in the form of complete rule making authority of the upper class versus no authority for the lower class. The units of analysis were the sixty-four societies. In the previous sections, the 128 social classes were treated as the units of analysis.

Number of Rule Changes

Various measures were used to predict the number of rule changes (see Figure 9-4). The most successful of these predictors was the size of the group. Seventeen percent ($r = -.41$, $p < .001$) of the variation in the number of rule changes was explained by the size of the group. Larger square groups seemed to have more difficulty coordinating their rule change procedures, so they made fewer rules. The pattern of partials (not shown) showed that group size predicted both perceptions of leadership at the end of Round 2 (discussed above) and the number of rule changes later in the game. Leadership was not an intervening variable between class size and the number of rule changes, as the zero order correlation of -.41 between size and the number of rule changes was the same as the partial correlation (controlling for leadership) between these two variables. The data did not support Hypotheses 2/3-1a, 2/3-1c, or 2/3-1d, but they did support Hypothesis 2/3-1b.

150

RULE CHANGE PORTION OF THE GAME BETWEEN ROUNDS 2 & 3

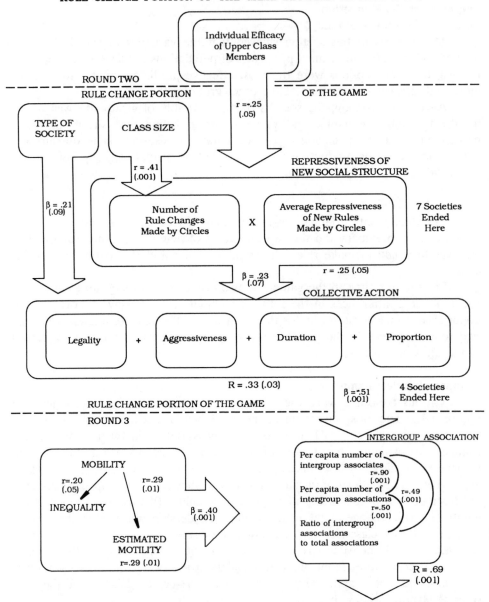

Figure 9-4: Diagram of Theory Model and Statistical Test for the Rule Change Portion of the Game

Repressiveness

Several sets of analyses (not shown) attempted to predict *maximum* and *average* repressiveness from other variables in the model. These analyses did not yield any strong or statistically significant relationships. Below, repressiveness will be combined with the number of rule changes in order to form a more complete index.

In only four of the sixty-four societies was the lower class triangle group the same or better off after the rule changes than before the changes took place. Generally speaking, giving the upper class squares complete authority to make rules was an advantage which they used to further their own group interests at the expense of the lower class triangles.

Results of the statistical analyses underscored the difficulty in predicting the number of rule changes and repressiveness of the rules. A clearer set of findings came from an analysis which took into account the total repressiveness of the new social structure. A measure of total repressiveness was created by multiplying the number of rule changes by the average repressiveness of the new rules. This operation had the same effect as simply adding up the repressiveness score of each separate rule change, but it was easier to compute given the way in which the data were coded. The analysis showed that the individual efficacy of upper class groups had a small effect upon the repressiveness of the new social structure. As efficacy increased by one standard deviation, repressiveness decreased by .25 standard deviation. Only about six percent of the variation in repressiveness ($r = -.25$, $p < .05$) was explained by variation in individual efficacy of upper class groups.

As upper class square groups were characterized by members who exhibited less efficacy, they tended to take group action against the lower class triangles by making repressive rules. Though the effects were small, they were statistically significant. Complete authority appeared to have such a strong effect on the game that the past history of societal openness or closure did not successfully predict any of the measures of repression. The data did not support Hypotheses 2/3-1d, 2/3-1e, 2/3-1g, 2/3-1h, or 2/3-1i, but they did support Hypothesis 2/3-1f.

The relative lack of predictability of repressiveness of the new rules pointed to at least two challenges for future research. First, it appeared that both concepts and measurements were weak in this area. Second, at least in STARPOWER, the rule making portion of the game was a time in which squares tried to come to grips with their new-found total authority. Much of the repression *emerged* during the process of rule making. This emergence should be studied more carefully without interfering with the autotelic nature of play. The processes should be examined both within and between groups. This research focused mostly on the processes that occurred *between* the groups.

VERBAL INTERACTIONS

The twelve categories of the Bales coding scheme were collapsed into four categories: positive emotions, declarative statements, questions, and negative emotions. Variables in the theoretical model generally were not predictive of verbal interactions (not shown). An exception to this overall pattern was the variable of *type of society*. In agrarian societies, triangles made more descriptive statements than they did in industrial societies ($r = -.29$, $p < .001$). In agrarian societies, squares tended to make more negative statements than they did in industrial societies ($r = -.35$, $p < .001$). The data supported Hypotheses 2/3-2a and 2/3-2c. The data did not support Hypothesis 2/3-2b.

In the agrarian societies, triangles were likely to tell squares that they ought to change some of the rules in order to improve conditions for the triangles. These petitions rarely were voiced in the form of questions. Typically, they were *statements* of the form, "Increase the trade bonus." In the agrarian societies, squares were trying to hang on to their advantages *as a group*. A typical response to a triangle statement concerning rule changes (if they answered at all) was "forget you!"

Predicting Verbal Interaction
From Interactions of the Other
Group (not shown)

Like rule changes that were discussed above, the interaction patterns emerged in the game. The interactions of each group tended to match those of the other. For instance, the number of positive statements made by triangles was correlated .53 ($p < .001$) with the number of positive statements made by squares. Likewise, the numbers of negative statements made by each group also were correlated ($r = .64$, $p < .001$).

For triangles, the interaction variables were more highly correlated with other interaction variables (average $r = .72$, $p < .001$) than they were with structural variables, perceptions, rule change variables, or interactions from the squares. The model did not explain which triangle groups attempted to use verbal interaction as a major method of trying to influence the square group.

For squares, social structural predictors, perceptions and other interactions were not predictive of interaction. In other words, verbal interaction was not used to try to convince the triangles of *anything*. After all, the squares had complete authority. They chose when (and how) to interact. They responded to some of the triangle questions and statements. They announced rule changes, and they reacted negatively to some triangle statements and negative interactions.

Though the data were not time-ordered, typical sequences went like this one: Positive interactions were met with positive responses ($r = .53$, $p < .001$). Triangle suggestions (statements) were evaluated negatively by squares ($r = .66$, $p < .001$). Negative interactions resulted in negative responses ($r = .64$, $p < .001$). Triangle questions were answered with square statements ($r = .57$, $p < .001$) or they simply were ignored! Square statements, either as answers to questions or as announcements about new rules, were met by triangle negative responses ($r = .66$, $p < .001$). Square questions usually represented attempts at responsiveness, and they were correlated with triangle positive interactions ($r = $

.35, p < .001). Also, a correlation was observed between triangle positive interaction and square negative interactions. Unsolicited good will on the part of triangles was taken as a sign of weakness, and it tended to be met with negative responses from squares. The data supported Hypotheses 2/3-2d through 2/3-2j.

Summary of the Analysis
Of Verbal Interaction

Interaction between the two social classes was predicted better by other *interactions* than it was by the other variables in the model, such as structural conditions, perceptions, or rule changes. One avenue for future research might involve the examination of each interaction in order to find out what kind of rule change or verbal interaction preceded it, and what followed it. In order for such a painstaking analysis to be fruitful, the interaction patterns must have shown themselves to be predictors of rule changes and collective action; however, in the next section it will be shown that interaction patterns did not successfully predict either of these processes.

COLLECTIVE ACTION

Severity of collective action was conceptualized as an index that was composed of dimensions of legality, aggressiveness, duration, and proportion of the group involved. The index of collective action was computed by adding-up the numerical values of each of the dimensions.

In four of the simulated societies, the collective action was severe enough that a third round of the game was never completed. All four of these societies were of the agrarian type.

In the prediction of severity of collective action, the type of society and total repressiveness by the squares were low in magnitude, but they were non-zero in their effects.

In industrial societies, collective action was .21 standard deviation less (p < .07) than it was in agrarian societies (see left center portion of Figure 9-4). As total repression increased by one standard deviation, collective action increased by .23 standard deviation (p < .07). Only eleven percent of the variation in collective action was explained (R = .33, p < .03) by the linear, additive combination of type of society and repressiveness of the new social structure.

In order to investigate further the ability of variables in the model to predict collective action, additional variables were added to the regression equation, even though their effects were small and not statistically significant. Collective action was extremely difficult to predict using the variables which were available within the model.

Müller (1985) showed that the relationship between regime repressiveness and political violence is best represented by a nonmonotonic inverted "U" function. This relationship was tested by a quadratic polynomial equation in which the repressiveness measure and its square were entered as predictors of the severity of collective action. If the relationship conformed to an inverted U curve, the beta for repressiveness would have a positive sign, and the beta for repressiveness squared would have a negative sign (Müller, 1985: 56). The data supported the inverted U-curve hypothesis slightly better than they supported the linear one (above).

A further check on the operation of the model involved the prediction of the separate components of collective action: 1) Legality, 2) Aggressiveness, 3) Duration, and 4) Proportion of Players involved. Results of this analysis (not shown) revealed a slightly different set of predictors for each of the components of collective action, but the *strength* of the relationships paralleled the analyses above. The data supported Hypotheses 2/3-3a. They supported a curvilinear version of Hypothesis 2/3-3c. The data did not support Hypothesis 2/3-3b or Hypotheses 2/3-3d through 2/3-3h.

Summary of Rule Changes
And Collective Action

Both rule making by the squares and collective action by the triangles had a spontaneous quality which limited the effectiveness of predictors which were measured at the end of the second round. The fact that the interaction patterns predicted neither rule changes nor collective action further underscored the emergent quality of this part of the simulation. Even though many of the conditions favoring collective action were present, its occurrence was by no means certain.

ROUND 3

Seven societies ended during the rule making. Four societies ended due to collective action. Two additional societies ended due to time limit problems that were not related to class conflict. Players in fifty-one of the sixty-four simulated societies played a third round of the game. The analysis of the third round of play in these fifty-one societies is summarized in Figure 9-5.

Status Characteristics

As in earlier rounds, characteristics of the social structure were used to predict status characteristics; however, none of them did. Apparently, the effects of social class, society type, and group size were overwhelmed by the emergent behavior of both squares and triangles. Status characteristics for Round 3 could not be predicted by variables in the model (see bottom left portion of Figure 9-4). The data did not support Hypothesis 3-1a.

As in earlier rounds of STARPOWER, increases in scores by a group (mobility) were predictive of the number of players who would have been motile had the game continued. The link between mobility and motility was weaker for the third round than for the other two rounds ($r = .29$ vs. $r = .45$ and $r = .51$). This finding indicated that overall, the social classes had replaced individuals as the primary actors in this part of the game. If one class was trading vigorously, the other class tended to follow suit. Under these conditions, both classes experienced mobility (increases in scores), but due to the fact that players brought forward their scores from Round 2 (reinvestment), the net effect was *less* motility than in previous rounds.

Also, for the first time in the game, mobility by a group as a whole led to inequality within the group. Though the effect was small (r = .20, p < .05) some players in the group worked very hard to gain points, thus raising the group average (mobility). This process, however, also created greater inequality within the group, as predicted by Blau. The data supported Hypothesis 3-1b, but they did not support Hypothesis 3-1c.

Intergroup Association

The interrelations among the three components of intergroup association were similar to those in previous rounds. The number of outgroup players with whom one traded (associates) and the number of outgroup trades (associations) remained highly correlated (r = .90). Neither of these variables was as highly correlated with the ratio of ingroup to outgroup associations (r = .50, r = .49) as it was in earlier rounds. These latter two correlations were higher than they were in the second round. In Round 3 trading returned to a pattern of exclusivity more like Round 1 than Round 2. The data supported Hypothesis 3-2a.

Forty-eight percent of the variation in patterns of association (R = .69, p < .001) was explained by the linear additive combination of triangle collective action and status characteristics. As collective action increased by one standard deviation, subsequent patterns of intergroup association decreased by .51 standard deviation (p < .001). Collective action that was aimed at furthering the interests of one's group decreased later associations that players made with members of the outgroup.

As status characteristics increased by one standard deviation, in Round 3 the patterns of outgroup association decreased by .40 standard deviation (p < .001). In the first round of the game, striving behavior was based on the type of society, and the relationship between status characteristics and intergroup association was a positive one; increases in striving led to increases in intergroup association. By Round 3, striving had become much more *class-based*, so that the greater was the increase in status, the less players interacted with members of the other class. Also, as the severity of collective action increased, the amount of intergroup association decreased. Quite simply, players came to rely more upon resources within their own group than upon those in the other group. The data did not support Hypotheses 3-2b, but they did support Hypotheses 3-2c and 3-2d.

Postgame Perceptions

Class size had a small effect upon class organization (see Figure 9-5). The larger was the group, the more the members perceived that they acted with conflicting plans of action (r = -.20, p < .001). Also, the greater was the group size, the less the members developed consensus on leadership (r = -.36 p < .001).

156

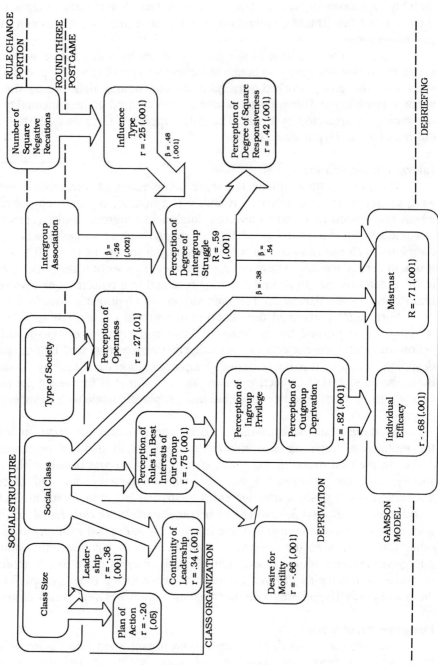

Figure 9-5: Diagram of Theory Model and Statistical Test for Postgame Perceptions

The data supported Hypotheses 3-3a and 3-3b, but they did not support Hypothesis 3-3c.

Social class had an effect upon the variable of continuity of leadership ($r = .34$, $p < .001$). Continuity of leadership was a dummy variable which was scored "1" when the player who got the most leadership votes in Round 2 was also the person who received the most votes at the end of play. Upper classes tended to have more continuity in this type of leadership than did lower classes. The data supported Hypothesis 3-4a.

In the earlier rounds of the game, leadership involved helping the group to follow the instructions of the game administrator. The upper classes could handle the task of changing the rules within the existing organizational framework. On the other hand, the lower class was required to change the group organization (at least in terms of leadership) in order to deal creatively with new contingencies created by the rule changes.

As expected, social class was a strong predictor of the extent to which a class felt that the rules were in its own best interests ($r = .75$, $p < .001$). This relationship was stronger at the end of the game than it was at the end of Round 2 ($r = .65$). Through bitter experience, players realized that the rule making privilege gave the upper class tremendous advantages in the game. The data supported Hypothesis 3-4b. The data did not support the direct effects of social class on desire for motility and perceived deprivation (Hypotheses 3-4c and 3-4d). Rather, the variable of rules in the best interests of our group intervened between social class and desire for motility, and it intervened between social class and deprivation. The data did not support Hypotheses 3-4e and 3-4f.

The variable of rules in the best interests of our group was a strong predictor of other perceptions, too. It predicted perceived deprivation ($r = .82$, $p < .001$) and desire for motility ($r = -.66$, $p < .001$). The data supported Hypotheses 3-5a and 3-5b. Upper classes perceived their own privilege, and they perceived the deprivation of the lower class in their society. They did not want to become members of the lower class. Likewise, lower classes were characterized by perceptions of ingroup deprivation and outgroup privilege, and many members of these classes desired upward motility.

Deprivation in turn was a strong predictor of feelings of individual efficacy ($r = .68$, $p < .001$). To the extent that a group felt that it was privileged (and that the other group was deprived), it was characterized by a feeling that its members could affect the behavior of the players in the other group.

The variables of perception of rules being in the best interests of one's group, deprivation, and individual efficacy were highly intercorrelated. The pattern of partial correlations was consistent with Figure 9-5.

Finally, social class was a predictor of mistrust. Upper classes were more mistrustful of lower classes than the reverse. The wording of the question, "Members of the other group cannot be trusted to do what *is right*" referred to rule governed behavior of the game more directly than it did to moral behavior in the real world. Due to the fact that upper class members made the rules, they didn't have to break them in the pursuit of their class interests. Therefore, lower class members were viewed as less trustworthy than were upper class members (beta = .38, p < .001).

The type of society had a small effect upon the perception that the basis of mobility was a result of individual endeavor (r = .27, p < .01). As expected, this relationship was weaker at the end of the game than it was at the end of Round 2 (r = .55) because the rules had changed. The fact that the relationship existed at all pointed to a tradition through which openness or closure of a society tended to form some basis for its future operation. The data supported Hypothesis 3-6.

Intergroup Association

Intergroup association had a small effect upon the perceptions of struggle between the two groups (beta = -.26, p < .002). Perception of intergroup struggle was predicted more directly from intergroup association than it was from collective action. The data did not support Hypotheses 3-7a, 3-7b, or 3-7c. The data did support Hypothesis 3-7d.

Group Interaction

The process of interaction between the two groups was predictive of other variables in the model. Specifically the greater the number of negative interactions that the lower class triangles directed at the upper class squares, the more likely both groups were to view attempts at influence as "threats of disadvantages" (beta = .56, p < .017; r = .25, p < .001). The data supported Hypothesis 3-8a.

These threats of disadvantages, in turn, predicted the degree of perceived intergroup struggle (beta = .48, p < .001). The combined effects of patterns of association (discussed above) and threats of disadvantages were predictive of perceived intergroup struggle (R = .59, p < .001). The data supported Hypothesis 3-8b. An interesting sidelight is that in the prediction of intergroup struggle, the variable of collective action competed unsuccessfully with the other two variables for entry into the prediction equation. Evidently, in the minds of players, negative interactions and subsequent lack of intergroup association were critical components of conflict. The term "discussion" as used in the item which measured this variable oriented respondents more to examples of interaction than it did to collective action. Thus, while collective action was related to perceptions of intergroup struggle (r = .38, p < .001; not shown), when the variables of influence type and patterns of intergroup association were controlled statistically, this relationship became quite small (beta = .13, N.S.). This finding suggests that in future research, the concept of collective action should include a more comprehensive set of measures than it did in this research.

Intergroup Struggle

Perception of intergroup struggle by members of a society was a predictor of the perceptions of responsiveness of the upper class members to suggestions from members of the lower class (r = .42, p < .001). Gamson (1974) found that groups which fought for what they wanted were more successful than those which did not. The findings for STARPOWER are consistent with this notion. The societies in which players perceived a greater degree of struggle were those in which players also perceived a greater degree of elite (square) responsiveness. The data supported Hypothesis 3-8c.

Intergroup struggle also predicted mistrust (beta = .54, p < .001). In fact, fifty percent of the variation in mistrust was explained by the linear additive combination of social class (discussed earlier) and intergroup struggle (R = .71, p < .001). The data supported Hypothesis 3-8d.

SUMMARY OF DATA ANALYSIS

The starting point for the quantitative data analysis was the examination of simulated agrarian and industrial societies. The aim of the analysis was to examine the relation between stratification and collective action.

In Round 1, industrial societies were characterized by greater mobility, inequality, and motility. In turn, higher values on these status characteristics and larger groups were characterized by greater intergroup association. Upper class members had less desire for motility than did members of the lower class. Also, they perceived greater openness of the social system. Greater intergroup association resulted in greater perception of openness. Group action, operationalized as the successful allocation of group bonus chips, could not be predicted by variables in the model.

By the second round of the game, upper classes were characterized by more mobility and inequality than were lower classes. (By definition, motility was equal for upper and lower classes.) As before, industrial societies were characterized by greater values on these status characteristics than were agrarian societies. Also, industrial societies were characterized by greater intergroup association. Group action was inhibited by a desire for motility and a feeling that motility could be gained through individual effort.

At the end of Round 2, information was gathered on perceptions of players. As players became more familiar with the society and their position in it, social class and type of society became more important predictors of other variables in the model than was intergroup association. Players began to operate on a more abstract and general level (a higher level of consciousness) than before.

During the rule change portion of the game, both repressiveness and collective action emerged as a result of the interaction of the groups. The forms of repression and collective action were completely free to vary, and as such, often they were highly creative responses to novel situations in the game. Because of the spontaneous quality of rule making and collective action--and because of the "loss" of the eleven most extreme societies--variables that appeared earlier in the model were not as highly predictive as before.

As an independent variable, the more severe was the collective action, the less frequent was the intergroup association. Group strategies (not measured) apparently washed out the effects of social class and type of society upon intergroup association. Repression was not predictive of subsequent status characteristics. Social classes became the most important entities in the simulation. Since the privilege of rule making was given to the upper class as a whole, and for the most part, social classes were the actors in the game, it is not surprising that social class became a strong predictor of perceptions.

Overall, the social structural variables of society type and social class were strong predictors of other aspects of the society such as status characteristics, intergroup association, and perceptions. Status characteristics were predictive only of intergroup association. Collective action proved itself to be a better independent variable than one that was dependent upon other variables in the model. In STARPOWER, collective action was difficult to predict, but its consequences were clear. Once severe collective action took place, intergroup association was never the same.

The use of multiple regression techniques may have obscured the central theme of this research, i.e., the effect of the type of society upon the collective action within it. The findings can be reviewed using simpler methods.

First, the giving of complete authority to upper class squares washed out the effects of just about everything which occurred prior to it in the game. Almost universally, the lower class triangles were repressed by the squares. In sixty out of the sixty-four societies the lower class triangles were worse off after the rule changes than before them.

Second, eleven simulated societies underwent drastic disruption. In four of them, the upper class squares completely repressed the lower class triangles by ending the game. Three of these societies were of the agrarian type, and one was of the industrial type. Three simulated societies failed to continue because of the internal collapse of the upper class square group. Two of the societies were of the industrial type, and one was an agrarian-type society. Four societies were brought to a halt as a result of disruptive collective action by the lower class triangles. All four of these societies were of the agrarian type.

Third, fifteen simulated societies continued a pattern which was reflective of the second round of play. This pattern was defined as one of "business as usual." Eleven of them began as industrial societies, and four began as agrarian societies. Nineteen industrial societies and nineteen agrarian societies exhibited patterns of conflict which were midway between the extremes of "drastic disruption" and "business as usual."

Finally, a cross-classification of the type of society with the type of change for the twenty-six societies which had the most extreme outcomes yielded a table such as the one presented in Table 9-1. The table shows that the type of society had important effects upon the type of change which it underwent. Only two of the eleven societies which underwent changes such as complete repression, elite collapse, or successful rebellion began as industrial societies. Nine of eleven societies which underwent these changes began as agrarian societies. The table also shows graphically that of the fifteen societies which continued with business

Type of Society

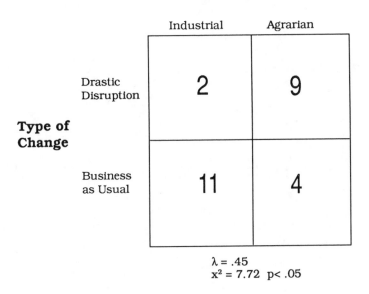

$$\lambda = .45$$
$$x^2 = 7.72 \quad p < .05$$

Table 9-1:   Cross classification of Type of Change in a Simulated Society by the Type of Society for the Twenty-six Societies Having the Most Extreme Outcomes

as usual, eleven began as industrial societies and only four began as agrarian societies. The relation between the type of society and the type of change is reasonably strong and statistically significant (Lambda = .45; $p \leq .05$).

Even in spite of repression in both types of societies, in those which began with a low level of technological efficiency and ascriptive status, classes more often became agents of conflict, and collective action was more dramatic when it occurred. In societies which began with a higher level of technological efficiency and achieved status, individuals competed with each other. Even in spite of elite repression, collective action in these societies was apt to be directed at replacement of the upper class through mobility rather than through more severe conflict. These findings should hold true for both real societies and for their simulated counterparts.

AFTERWORD

Research with sixty-four ideal type industrial and agrarian societies in the "world apart" of the STARPOWER simulation resulted in "seeing more clearly" (p. 3) the relation between the type of society and collective action. Some of the observations resulted directly from the game. Others came from the theorists who provided the theoretical model. Observations also came from qualitative and quantitative analyses of the data that was generated by players.

1. Due to a more advanced technology, industrial society produces more value for a given amount of labor than does agrarian society.

2. Individuals in industrial society have greater opportunity for achievement than they do in agrarian society.

3. Individual competition is more important for achievement in industrial society than it is in agrarian society.

4. The system of stratification in industrial society creates more mobility, inequality and motility than that of agrarian society.

6. Industrial society has greater intergroup association (macrosocial integration) than does agrarian society.

7. In industrial society individuals attribute success or failure to themselves. In agrarian society, if they have attempted to achieve upward mobility-- and if they have failed--they attribute failure to the system of stratification.

8. A greater number of decision makers have been upwardly motile in industrial society than in agrarian society.

9. In industrial society decisions are made by a class of individuals who have *achieved* the highest status positions. In agrarian society decisions are made by a class of individuals who have been *ascribed* the highest status positions.

10. Giving complete authority to make decisions to a class will result in decisions that favor that class.

11. Collective action requires individuals to believe that they must act together in conflict with another group to achieve a collective goal.

12. Fusion, a type of collective action, is an expression of freedom. It is a temporary merging of the individual and the other.

13. Fusion requires structural conditions that allow it. Individuals express their freedom through others, so fusion is difficult to predict.

14. To continue collective action, the "conflict group" must organize itself. This organization constrains individual freedom, so fusion cannot be maintained.

15. Organization of a conflict group requires the giving up of individual freedom, and it requires effort on the part of group members, so it too is difficult to predict.

16. Industrial society is more tolerant of repression than is agrarian society.

17. Since industrial society is based on *individual* competition, drastic collective action is less likely than it is in agrarian society.

18. Collective action decreases intergroup association (macrosocial integration) because a group has acted as an agent of conflict.

Certainly these observations could be derived from other types of research, so what has this research accomplished? When Harold Guetzkow was asked the same question about research with the Inter-Nation Simulation (INS) and Simulated International Processes (SIP), he replied,

> Let me be reckless: the . . . field is "better off". . . Simulations permit one to tackle immense problems of great complexity, involving large numbers of variables . . . Nevertheless, we realize that simulation is but one of the array of tools with which we gain "better" coherence as we accumulate knowledge in the field of international affairs (Guetzkow and Valdez, 1981: 331-332).

The contribution of research with STARPOWER to the field of collective action generally is the same as that cited by Guetzkow, but the magnitude of the contribution is less. The implications of research with STARPOWER are the following ones:

1) There is a place in the classroom for cooperative investigations by teachers and students. Experience in the field of gamed simulation over the last twenty-five years has shown that "fun" and the play spirit are compatible with social science research.

2) The modifications to the game allowed the investigation of ideal-type agrarian and industrial societies, even though no ideal-type society ever has existed in the real world. The investigation was possible because of three things: First, the simulation abstracted only the stratification system of society. Second, the simulation substituted a very short period of time for a long term process. It was but a few feet of film from a very long movie. Third, the simulation used smaller groups to stand for much larger ones. These characteristics were used to great advantage in bringing society into the classroom. They allowed for many replications to be made under controlled conditions, and they allowed both qualitative and quantative techniques to be used in gathering data.

3) The combination of simulation and classroom setting allowed for the examination of *micro* processes ("patterned interaction among individuals;" see Münch and Smelser, 1987: 357) and *macro* processes ("structures of society;" see Münch and Smelser, 1987: 357). The research offered an example of how to bridge the micro-macro gulf. The reasonably good fit between theory that was developed for the "real world" and STARPOWER is evidence for the validity of the simulation.

4) The whole conception of STARPOWER and of the theory model implied a causal process, yet the modeling of these processes still is very imprecise. Since knowledge about stratification systems and collective action is characterized by low clarity and low consensus, much work still needs to be done on the relationships among variables and whether processes can be conceptualized more effectively as deterministic or stochastic. Nevertheless, the research brought together various divergent strands of theory in the study of collective action; thus we can "see better."

What then of future research with STARPOWER? The two versions of the game mirrored in a very abstract way the essential features of stratification systems which were characteristic of societies of the agrarian and industrial types. If Bell (1973), Toffler (1980), Naisbitt (1984) and others are correct, countries in Western Europe, North America and Asia are moving toward post-industrial society. The transition will be at least as profound as the one from agrarian to industrial society (Naisbitt, 1984: 9). Postindustrialism will be based on information, a resource that is mass-produced and self-renewing. Naisbitt argues,

In an information economy, then, value is increased, not by labor, but by knowledge (Naisbitt, 1984: 8).

Who will produce this knowledge? How will it be distributed? Naisbitt implies that it will be shared because it is most powerful when it is in the hands of the many. Couldn't it be used for personal gain if it remained private? Wouldn't producers have a greater claim to it than those who merely consumed it? In agrarian society, resources were fixed in value. In industrial class systems resources were highly responsive to investment of time and effort in them. How will information society operate? As postindustrialism unfolds (if it does at all), STARPOWER would seem to be an appropriate vehicle for the study of stratification and collective action within this new "world apart." Perhaps some future social science student will take part in a reenactment of a critical moment in history in which non-technocrats "storm the Bastille."

APPENDIX A

SAMPLE SCORESHEET

PLAYER'S LOG: ROUND 1

Please enter the number or letter on your identification tag here

For each trade that you complete, enter the number or letter of the person with whom you traded in one of the boxes below.

Total value of chips you now have ☐ + Bonus for same colors ☐ + Bonus for number of trades ☐ = ☐ Score you give to Game Director

+ Group Bonus (if any) ☐ = TOTAL SCORE FOR ROUND 1 ☐ Carry this score to Round 2

Now that you have played one round of the game we would like to find out your reactions to play of the game. Answer as you <u>now</u> feel.

Please check the appropriate blank as follows:
<u>A</u> = strongly agree; <u>a</u> = agree; <u>U</u> = uncertain; <u>d</u> = disagree; <u>D</u> = strongly disagree

1. If I had a chance I would like to become a member of the other group.

     A   a   U   d   D
   1   2   3   4   5

2. A square can become a circle if he really tries.

     A   a   U   d   D
   1   2   3   4   5

ROUND 2:

Please enter the number or letter of the tag you are <u>NOW</u> wearing here. ☐

For each trade you complete enter the number or letter of the person with whom you traded in one of the boxes below.

Total from last round ☐ + Total value of chips you now have ☐ + Bonus for same colors ☐ + Bonus for number of trades ☐ =

Score you give to Game Director ☐ + Group Bonus (if any) ☐ = TOTAL SCORE FOR ROUND 2 ☐ Carry this score to next round if indicated

Now that you have played two rounds of the game we would like to find out your reactions to play of the game. Answer as you <u>now</u> feel.

Please check the appropriate blank as follows:
<u>A</u> = strongly agree; <u>a</u> = agree; <u>U</u> = uncertain; <u>d</u> = disagree; <u>D</u> = strongly disagree

1. If I had a chance I would like to become a member of the other group.

   __A   __a   __U   __d   __D
    1   2   3   4   5

2. A triangle can become a square if he really tries.

   __A   __a   __U   __d   __D
    1   2   3   4   5

3. The game rules are in the best interests of our group.

   __A   __a   __U   __d   __D
    1   2   3   4   5

4. Players like me don't have any say about what the other group does.

   __A   __a   __U   __d   __D
    1   2   3   4   5

5. Even if players like us act together, we can't have much effect on what the other group does.

   __A   __a   __U   __d   __D
    1   2   3   4   5

6. The other group can't be trusted to do what is right.

   __A   __a   __U   __d   __D
    1   2   3   4   5

7. How would you describe your present situation in the game? (Check one)

Best possible __ __ __ __ __ __ __ Worst possible
              1   2   3   4   5   6   7

8. How would you describe <u>present</u> situation of the <u>other group</u>?

Best possible ___ ___ ___ ___ ___ ___ ___ Worst possible
               1   2   3   4   5   6   7

9. Who is the player who has done the most to help your group move toward its goals?

    ____ (Enter his/her tag number or letter here)

10. Our group operates with sets of conflicting plans.

   ___A   ___a   ___U   ___d   ___D
    1   2   3   4   5

ROUND 3:

Please enter the number or letter of the tag you are <u>NOW</u> wearing here. ☐

For each trade you complete enter the number or letter of the person with whom you traded in one of the boxes below.

Total from last round ☐ + Total value of chips you now have ☐ + Bonus for same colors ☐ + Bonus for number of trades ☐ =

Score you give to Game Director ☐ + Group Bonus (if any) ☐ = TOTAL SCORE ☐

Now that you have played three rounds of the game we would like to find out your reactions to play of the game. Answer as you <u>now</u> feel.

Please check the appropriate blank as follows:
<u>A</u> = strongly agree; <u>a</u> = agree; <u>U</u> = uncertain; <u>d</u> = disagree; <u>D</u> = strongly disagree

1. If I had a chance I would like to become a member of the other group.

   ___A   ___a   ___U   ___d   ___D
    1   2   3   4   5

2. A triangle can become a square if he really tries.

   ___A   ___a   ___U   ___d   ___D
    1   2   3   4   5

3. The game rules are in the best interests of our group.

   ___A   ___a   ___U   ___d   ___D
    1   2   3   4   5

4. Players like me don't have any say about what the other group does.

   ___A   ___a   ___U   ___d   ___D
    1   2   3   4   5

5. Even if players like us act together, we can't have much effect on what the other group does.

   ___A   ___a   ___U   ___d   ___D
    1   2   3   4   5

6. The other group can't be trusted to do what is right.

   ___A   ___a   ___U   ___d   ___D
    1   2   3   4   5

7. How would you describe your present situation in the game? (Check one)

Best possible ___ ___ ___ ___ ___ ___ ___ Worst possible
                1   2   3   4   5   6   7

8. How would you describe <u>present</u> situation of the <u>other group</u>?

Best possible $\frac{\underline{\quad}}{1} \quad \frac{\underline{\quad}}{2} \quad \frac{\underline{\quad}}{3} \quad \frac{\underline{\quad}}{4} \quad \frac{\underline{\quad}}{5} \quad \frac{\underline{\quad}}{6} \quad \frac{\underline{\quad}}{7}$ Worst possible

9. Who is the player who has done the most to help your group move toward its goals?

____ (Enter his/her tag number or letter here)

10. Our group operates with sets of conflicting plans.

$\frac{\underline{\quad}A}{1} \qquad \frac{\underline{\quad}a}{2} \qquad \frac{\underline{\quad}U}{3} \qquad \frac{\underline{\quad}d}{4} \qquad \frac{\underline{\quad}D}{5}$

11. What is the best description of how the other group tried to influence us?

____They tried to influence us without offering us any advantages or
1 threatening any disadvantages.

____They tried to influence us by offering us advantages.
2

____They tried to influence us by threatening us with disadvantages.
3

12. What is the best description of relations between the groups during this last round?

Peaceful   Militant
Discussion $\quad \underline{\quad} \qquad \underline{\quad} \qquad \underline{\quad} \qquad \underline{\quad} \qquad \underline{\quad}$ Struggle

$\qquad\qquad\quad 1 \qquad\quad 2 \qquad\quad 3 \qquad\quad 4 \qquad\quad 5$

13. How many of the triangles' proposals were incorporated into the rules by the squares?

All $\quad \frac{\underline{\quad}}{1} \qquad \frac{\underline{\quad}}{2} \qquad \frac{\underline{\quad}}{3} \qquad \frac{\underline{\quad}}{4} \qquad \frac{\underline{\quad}}{5}$ None

REFERENCES

Acock, Alan C. and Melvin L. DeFleur. (1972). "A configurational approach to contingent consistency in the attitude-behavior relationship." *American Sociological Review* 37 (December): 714-726.

Allison, Paul D. (1978). "Measures of inequality." *American Sociological Review* 43 (December): 865-880.

Almond, Gabriel and Sidney Verba. (1963). *The Civic Culture.* Princeton, NJ: Princeton University Press.

Andrews, Kenneth H. and Denise B. Kandel. (1979). "Attitude and behavior: a specification of the contingent consistency hypothesis." *American Sociological Review* 44 (April): 298-310.

Ashton, Thomas Southcliffe. (1948). *The Industrial Revolution, 1760-1830.* London: Oxford Press.

Auman, Robert A. (1988). *Notes on Game Theory.* Boulder, CO: Westview Press.

BAFA' BAFA'. (1974). R. Garry Shirts. Del Mar, CA: Simile II.

Bales, Robert F. (1950). *Interaction Process Analysis: A Method for the Study of Small Groups.* Reading, MA: Addison-Wesley.

Bales, Robert F. (1970). *Personality and Interpersonal Behavior.* New York: Holt, Rinehart and Winston.

Barney, Gerald O. (1980). *The Global 2000 Report to the President*, Vol. 1. Washington, D.C.: U.S. Government Printing Office.

Bell, Daniel. (1973). *The Coming of Post Industrial Society.* New York: Basic Books.

Berger, Peter L. *(1986) The Capitalist Revolution.* New York: Basic Books.

Berne, Eric. (1964). *Games People Play.* New York: Grove Press.

178

Bierstedt, Robert. (1959). "Nominal and real definitions in sociological theory," pp. 121-144 in L. Gross (ed.) *Symposium on Sociological Theory*, New York: Harper and Row.

Black, Donald. (1976). *The Behavior of Law*. New York: Academic Press.

Blau, Peter. (1977). *Inequality and Heterogeneity*. New York: Free Press.

Blalock, Hubert M., Jr. (1969). *Theory Construction*. Englewood Cliffs, NJ: Prentice Hall.

Boocock, Sarane S. (1972). "Validity-testing of an intergenerational relations game." *Simulation and Games* 3 (March): 29-40.

Boocock, Sarane S. and E. O. Schild. (1969). GENERATION GAP. Indianapolis, IN: Bobbs Merrill Co.

Bredemeier, Mary E. and Cathy Stein Greenblat. (1981). "The educational effectiveness of simulation games: a synthesis of findings. *Simulation and Games* 12 (September): 307-332.

Brody, Richard A. (1963). "Some systemic effects of nuclear weapons technology: a study through simulation of a multi-nuclear future." *Journal of Conflict Resolution*, 7: 633-753.

Brody, Richard, Alexandra Benham and Jeffrey Milstein. (1966). "Hostile international communication, arms production, and perception of threat: a simulation study. Stanford, CA: Institute of Political Studies, Stanford University.

Bwy, Douglas. (1968). "Dimension of social conflict in Latin America." *American Behavioral Scientist* 11 (March-April): 39-50.

Coleman, James S. (1961). *The Adolescent Society*. New York: The Free Press.

Coleman, James S. (1968a). "Games as Vehicles for Social Theory." Baltimore, MD: Johns Hopkins University Center for Social Organization of Schools Report 22.

Coleman, James S. (1968b). "Preface" and "Social Processes and Social Simulation Games." Pp. 7-10; 29-51 in S. Boocock and E. O. Schild (eds.), *Simulation Games in Learning*. Beverly Hills, CA: Sage Publication.

Coleman, James S. and Constance J. Seidner. (1972). HIGH SCHOOL. Unpublished simulation available from C. J. Seidner, 42 Willow Road., Sudbury, MA 01776.

Coppard, Larry and Fredrick Goodman (eds.). (1977). *Urban Gaming/Simulation '77.* Ann Arbor, MI: University of Michigan School of Education.

Crow, Wayman J. and John R. Raser. (1964). "A cross-cultural simulation study." La Jolla, CA: Western Behavior Sciences Institute.

Davis, James A. (1975). *Elementary Survey Analysis.* Englewood Cliffs, NJ: Prentice-Hall.

Davis, Morton D. (1983). *Game Theory.* Rev. Ed. New York: Basic Books.

Dahrendorf, Ralf. (1959). *Class and Class Conflict in Industrial Society.* Stanford, CA: Stanford University Press.

Deutcher, Irwin. (1973). *What We Say/What We Do.* Glenview, IL: Scott Foresman.

Domhoff, G. William. (1967). *Who Rules America?* Englewood Cliffs, NJ: Prentice-Hall, Inc.

Domhoff, G. William. (1970). *The Higher Circles.* New York: Vintage.

Driver, Michael. (1965). "A structural analysis of aggression, stress and personality in an inter-nation simulation. Lafayette, IN: Purdue University.

Druckman, Daniel. (1968) "Ethnocentrism in the inter-nation simulation." *Journal of Conflict Resolution* 12, 45-68.

Dukes, Richard L. (1974). "A test of multivariate model in two types of simulated social systems." *Simulation and Games* 5 (March): 23-46.

Dukes, Richard L. and Constance J. Seidner. (1973). "Self-role incongruence and role enactment in simulation games." *Simulation and Games* 4 (June): 159-173.

Dukes, Richard L. and Christine L. Mattley. (1986). "The effects of social structure and mobility on attitudes and behavior in a simulated society." *Simulation and Games* 17 (December): 467-484.

Dunphy, Dexter C. (1972). *The Primary Group: A Handbook for Analysis and Field Research*. New York: Appleton-Century-Crofts.

Durkheim, Emile. (1933). *The Division of Labor in Society*. New York: The Free Press of Glencoe.

Easton, David. (1953). *The Political System*. New York: Alfred A. Knopf, Inc.

Easton, Ralph. (1933). *General Logic*. New York: Charles Scribner's Sons.

Gamson, William A., Bruce Fireman, and Steven Rytina. (1982). *Encounters with Unjust Authority*. Homewood, IL: The Dorsey Press.

Gamson, William A. (1978). *SIMSOC, Simulated Society: Coordinators Manual*, 3d. ed., New York: The Free Press.

Gamson, William A. (1975). *The Strategy of Social Protest*. Homewood, IL: The Dorsey Press.

Gamson, William A. (1968). *Power and Discontent*. Homewood, IL: The Dorsey Press.

Gardner, Ralph Jr. (1984). *Young, Gifted and Rich*. New York: Simon and Schuster.

Gerth, H. H. and C. Wright Mills (eds.). (1946). *From Max Weber*. New York: Oxford University Press.

GHETTO. (1969). Dove Toll, New York: Western Publishing Company.

Giddens, Anthony. (1973). *The Class Structure of Advanced Societies*. New York: Barnes and Noble.

Greenblat, Cathy Stein. (1988). *Designing Games and Simulations*. Newbury Park, CA: Sage Publications.

Guetzkow, Harold and Joseph J. Valdez. (1981). *Simulated International Processes: Theories and Research in Global Modelling*. Beverly Hills, CA: Sage Publications.

Guetzkow, Harold, Chadwock F. Alger, Richard A. Brody, Robert C. Noel, and Richard C. Synder. (1963). *Simulation in International Relations*. Englewood Cliffs, NJ: Prentice-Hall.

Gurr, Ted Robert. (1970). *Why Men Rebel.* Princeton, NJ: Princeton University Press.

Hardin, Garrett J. (1968). "The Tragedy of the Commons." *Science* 162: 1243-1248.

Hayim, Gila J. (1980). *The Existential Sociology of Jean-Paul Sartre.* Amherst, MA: University of Massachusetts Press.

Hermann, Charles F. (1972). "Threat, time, and surprise: A simulation of international crisis." Pp. 187-211 in Charles F. Hermann, ed., *International Crises: Insights From Behavioral Research.* New York: Free Press.

Hermann, Charles F. and Margaret G. Hermann. (1967). "An attempt to simulate the outbreak of World War I." *American Political Science Review* 61: 400-416.

Hobsbawm, Eric J. (1962). *The Age of Revolution, 1789-1848.* New York: New American Library.

Horn, Robert E. and Anne Cleaves (eds.). (1980). *The Guide to Simulations/ Games for Education and Training,* 3rd ed., Vol.1. Lexington, MA: Didactic Systems, Inc.

Huizinga, Johann. (1955). *Homo Ludens: A Study of the Play Element in Culture.* Boston: Beacon Press.

Inbar, Michael and Clarice S. Stoll. (1970). "Games and Learning." *Interchange:* 53-61.

Inbar, Michael. (1970). "Toward a sociology of autotelic behavior." *La Critica Sociologica* 14 (Summer) no page numbers.

Jones, Edward E. and Harold B. Gerard. (1967). *Foundations of Social Psychology.* New York: John Wiley and Sons, Inc.

Kim, Jae-On and Frank J. Kohout. (1975). "Special topics in general linear models." Pp. 368-397 in Norman H. Nie, *et al., SPSS: Statistical Package for the Social Sciences,* 2d. ed. New York: McGraw-Hill Book Company.

Kuhn, Thomas. (1970). *The Structure of Scientific Revolutions,* 2nd ed. Chicago: The University of Chicago Press.

Landecker, Werner S. (1989). *Class Crystallization.* New Brunswick, NJ: Rutgers University Press.

182

Lauffer, Armand. (1973). *The Aim of the Game.* Ann Arbor, MI: Gamed Simulations, Inc.

Lenski, Gerhard E. (1966). *Power and Privilege: A Theory of Social Stratification.* New York: McGraw-Hill Book Company.

Liska, A. (1974). "Emergent issues in the attitude-behavior consistency controversy." *American Sociological Review* 39 (April): 261-272.

Livingston, Samuel A., Gail M. Fennessey, James S. Coleman, Keith J. Edwards, Steven J. Kidder. (1973). "The Hopkins Games Program: Final Report on Seven Years of Research." Report No. 155. Baltimore, MD: Johns Hopkins University Center for Social Organization of Schools.

Long, Norton. (1958). "The local community as an ecology of games." *American Journal of Sociology* (November): 251-256.

Lundberg, Ferdinand. (1968). *The Rich and the Super-rich.* New York: Bantam.

Marx, Karl. (1956). Selected writings in sociology and social philosophy. Translated by T. B. Bottomore. New York: McGraw-Hill.

McCain, Garvin and Erwin M. Segal. (1969). *The Game of Science.* Belmont, CA: Brooks/Cole Publishing Company.

Meadows, Donella H., Dennis L. Meadows, Jorgen Randers, and William W. Behrens III. (1972). *The Limits to Growth: A Report for the Club of Rome's Project on the Predicament of Mankind.* 2d ed. New York: Signet.

Mesarovic, Mihajlo and Eduard Pestel. (1974). *Mankind at the Turning Point: The Second Report to the Club of Rome.* New York: Dutton.

Mills, C. Wright. (1956). *The Power Elite.* London: Oxford University Press.

Muller, Edward N. (1985). "Income inequality, regime repressiveness, and political violence." *American Sociological Review* 50 (February): 47-61.

Münch, Richard and Neil J. Smelser. (1987). "Relating the micro and macro," pp. 356-387 in Jeffery C. Alexander, Bernhard Giesen, Richard Münch, and Neil J. Smelser (eds.), *The Micro-Macro Link.* Berkeley, CA: University of California Press.

Naisbitt, John. (1984). *Megatrends.* New York: Warner Books.

Offe, Klaus. (1985). *Disorganized Capitalism.* Cambridge, MA: MIT Press.

Olson, Mancur. (1971). *The Logic of Collective Action.* Cambridge, MA: Harvard University Press.

Paige, Jeffery M. (1971). "Political orientation and riot participation." *American Sociological Review* 36 (October): 810-820.

Phillips, Derek L. (1973). *Abandoning Method.* San Francisco, CA: Jossey-Bass.

Plummer, Charles M. (1976). "Design and research of a simulation/game to operationalize 'Future Shock.'" Paper presented at the Annual Meetings of the North American Simulation and Gaming Association. Raleigh, North Carolina (October).

Powers, Richard B. (1985). "Cooperation, exploitation, or withdrawal from small and large commons." Paper presented at the Annual Meetings of the American Psychological Association, Los Angeles, CA, August.

Powers, Richard B. and William Boyle. (1983). "Generalization from a commons-dilemma game: the effects of a fine option, information, and communication on cooperation and defection." *Simulation and Games* 14 (September): 253-274.

Powers, Richard B., Richard E. Duus and Richard S. Norton. (1980). THE COMMONS GAME. Logan, UT: Utah State University.

Raser, John D. (1969). *Simulation and Society.* Boston: Allyn and Bacon.

Robinson, W. S. (1957). "The statistical measurement of agreement." *American Sociological Review* 22 (February): 17-25.

Russell, Constance J. (1972). "Simulating the adolescent society." *Simulation and Games* 3 (June): 165-188.

Russell, D. E. H. (1974). *Rebellion, Revolution, and Armed Force.* New York: Academic Press, Inc.

Schuman, Howard and Michael P. Johnson. (1976). "Attitudes and behavior." Pp. 161-207 in Alex Inkeles, *et al.* (eds.), *Annual Review of Sociology,* Vol. 2. Palo Alto, CA: Annual Reviews.

184

Seidner, Constance J. (1978). "Teaching with simulations and games." Pp. 11-45 in Richard L. Dukes and Constance J. Seidner (eds.), *Learning with Simulations and Games.* Beverly Hills, CA: Sage Publications.

Seidner, Constance J. and Richard L. Dukes. (1976). "Simulation in social psychological research: A methodological approach to the study of attitudes and behavior." *Simulation and Games* 77 (March): 3-20.

Sennett, Richard and Jonathan Cobb. (1972). *The Hidden Injuries of Class.* New York: Vantage Books.

Shirts, R. Garry. (1969/1974). *STARPOWER.* Del Mar, CA: SIMILE II. (P.O. Box 910, Zip 92014)

Silver, Burton. (1974). "Group success and personal commitment in game simulations." *Simulation and Games* 5 (December): 415-424.

Silver, Burton. (1973). "Social mobility and intergroup antagonism." *Journal of Conflict Resolution* 17 (December): 605-623.

SIMSOC, Simulated Society, 3d. ed. (1978). William Gamson. New York: Free Press.

Smelser, Neil J. (1962). *Theory of Collective Behavior.* New York: The Free Press.

Stoll, Clarice S. and Paul T. McFarlane. (1969). "Player characteristics and interaction in a parent-child simulation game." *Sociometry* 32 (September): 259-272.

Suits, Bernard. (1967). "What is a game?" *Philosophy of Science* 34: 148-158.

Sullivan, Denis G. with Robert Noel. (1972). "Inter-nation simulation: A review of its premises." Pp. 111-124 in Michael Inbar and Clarice S. Stoll (eds.), *Simulation and Gaming in Social Science.*

Tilly, Charles. (1978). *From Mobilization to Revolution.* Reading, MA: Addison-Wesley Publishing Company.

Toffler, Alvin. (1980). *The Third Wave.* New York: Bantam.

Toffler, Alvin. (1970). *Future Shock.* New York: Bantam.

Turner, Jonathan H. (1984). *Societal Stratification.* New York: Columbia University Press.

Turner, Ralph and Lewis M. Killian, eds. (1972). *Collective Behavior,* 2d. ed. Englewood Cliffs, NJ: Prentice-Hall, Inc.

Useem, Michael. (1975). *Protest Movements in America.* Indianapolis, IN: Bobbs-Merrill Company, Inc.

Van den Berghe, Pierre L. (1967). *Race and Racism: A Comparative Perspective.* New York: John Wiley and Sons, Inc.

Weber, Max. (1968). *Economy and Society* (3 volumes). New York: Bedminster Press.

Wicker, A. W. (1969). "Attitudes versus actions: The relationship of verbal and overt behavior responses to attitude objects." *Journal of Social Issues* 25: 41-78.

Willer, David. (1967). *Scientific Sociology.* Englewood Cliffs, NJ: Prentice-Hall, Inc.

Willer, David and George K. Zollschan. (1964). *Explorations in Social Change.* Boston: Houghton Mifflin.

Wolf, C. P. (1972). "SIMCANSOC: Simulated Canadian society. *Simulation and Games* 3 (March): 53-77.

Zetterberg, Hans. (1965). *On Theory and Verification in Sociology,* 3d. ed. Totowa, NJ: The Bedminster Press.

Zimmermann, Ekkart. (1983). *Political Violence, Crisis and Revolution: Theories and Research.* Rochester, VT: Schenkman.

Zinnes, Dina A. (1966). "A comparison of hostile state behavior in simulate and historical data." *World Politics* 18: 474-502.

THEORY AND DECISION LIBRARY

SERIES A: PHILOSOPHY AND METHODOLOGY OF THE SOCIAL
SCIENCES

Already published:

Conscience: An Interdisciplinary View
Edited by Gerhard Zecha and Paul Weingartner
ISBN 90–277–2452–0

Cognitive Strategies in Stochastic Thinking
by Roland W. Scholz
ISBN 90–277–2454–7

Comparing Voting Systems
by Hannu Nurmi
ISBN 90–277–2600–0

Evolutionary Theory in Social Science
Edited by Michael Schmid and Franz M. Wuketits
ISBN 90–277–2612–4

The Metaphysics of Liberty
by Frank Forman
ISBN 0–7923–0080–7

Principia Economica
by Georges Bernard
ISBN 0–7923–0186–2

Towards a Strategic Management and Decision Technology
by John W. Sutherland
ISBN 0–7923–0245–1

Social Decision Methodology for Technological Projects
Edited by Charles Vlek and George Cvetkovich
ISBN 0–7923–0371–7

Reductionism and Systems Theory in the Life Sciences
Edited by Paul Hoyningen-Huene and Franz M. Wuketits
ISBN 0–7923–0375–X

Understanding Economic Behaviour
Edited by Klaus G. Grunert and Folke Ölander
ISBN 0–7923–0482–9

The Lifetime of a Durable Good
by Gerrit Antonides
ISBN 0–7923–0574–4